THE FOOD & COOKING OF
FINLAND

THE FOOD & COOKING OF
FINLAND

Traditions ■ Ingredients ■ Tastes ■ Techniques ■ Over 60 Classic Recipes

ANJA HILL

with photographs by Martin Brigdale

aquamarine

This edition is published by Aquamarine
an imprint of Anness Publishing Ltd
Hermes House, 88–89 Blackfriars Road
London SE1 8HA
tel. 020 7401 2077
fax 020 7633 9499

www.aquamarinebooks.com;
www.annesspublishing.com

If you like the images in this book and would
like to investigate using them for publishing,
promotions or advertising, please visit our
website www.practicalpictures.com for
more information.

UK agent: The Manning Partnership Ltd;
tel. 01225 478444; fax 01225 478440;
sales@manning-partnership.co.uk

UK distributor: Book Trade Services;
tel. 0116 2759086; fax 0116 2759090;
uksales@booktradeservices.com;
exportsales@booktradeservices.com

North American agent/distributor:
National Book Network; tel. 301 459 3366;
fax 301 429 5746; www.nbnbooks.com

Australian agent/distributor:
Pan Macmillan Australia;
tel. 1300 135 113; fax 1300 135 103
customer.service@macmillan.com.au

New Zealand agent/distributor:
David Bateman Ltd; tel. (09) 415 7664
fax (09) 415 8892

Publisher: Joanna Lorenz
Senior Managing Editor: Conor Kilgallon
Project Editor: Lucy Doncaster
Designer: Simon Daley
Illustrator: Anthony Duke
Photography: Martin Brigdale
Food Stylist: Fergal Connolly
Prop Stylist: Helen Trent
Production Manager: Steve Lang

© Anness Publishing Ltd 2007, 2009

Ethical Trading Policy

Because of our ongoing ecological
investment programme, you, as our
customer, can have the pleasure and
reassurance of knowing that a tree is being
cultivated on your behalf to naturally replace
the materials used to make the book you
are holding. For further information about
this scheme, go to
www.annesspublishing.com/trees

Publisher's Note

Notes

Bracketed terms are intended for
American readers.

For all recipes, quantities are given in both
metric and imperial measures and, where
appropriate, in standard cups and spoons.
Follow one set of measures, but not a mixture,
because they are not interchangeable.

Standard spoon and cup measures are
level. 1 tsp = 5ml, 1 tbsp = 15ml,
1 cup = 250ml/8fl oz.

Australian standard tablespoons are 20ml.
Australian readers should use 3 tsp in place
of 1 tbsp for measuring small quantities of
gelatine, flour, salt, etc.

American pints are 16fl oz/2 cups. American
readers should use 20fl oz/2.5 cups in place
of 1 pint when measuring liquids.

Electric oven temperatures in this book are for
conventional ovens. When using a fan oven,
the temperature will probably need to be
reduced by about 10–20°C/20–40°F. Since
ovens vary, you should check with your
manufacturer's instruction book for guidance.

The nutritional analysis given for each recipe
is calculated per portion (i.e. serving or item),
unless otherwise stated. If the recipe gives a
range, such as Serves 4–6, then the
nutritional analysis will be for the smaller
portion size, i.e. 6 servings. Measurements
for sodium do not include salt added to taste.

Medium (US large) eggs are used unless
otherwise stated.

The very young, the elderly, pregnant
women and those in ill-health or with a
compromised immune system are advised
against consuming dishes containing raw
eggs, meat or fish.

Front cover shows Cep Mushroom Soup
(see page 26).

Contents

The Finnish landscape

Finland lies to the east of the Scandinavian peninsula. Between an 830-mile Russian border on one side and the Baltic Sea coast of 775 miles on the other, the terrain is made up largely of forest and lakes. While spruce and pine forests occupy 70 per cent of the land, water takes up about 10 per cent, and the rest is mainly farmed land. Long, dark winters and bright, hot summers characterize the climate that, along with the terrain, moulds a country that has retained its culinary traditions despite the advent of commercial imports from the rest of the world.

The landscape of Finland – shaped by the relatively recent (in geological terms) recession of continental glaciers 10,000 years ago – has several notable natural features, including an undulating rather than mountainous terrain, innumerable lakes and rivers, and 180,000 offshore islands, which comprise Europe's largest archipelago. Lying off the south-western coast, this group of islands include the Åland islands (Ahvenanmaa in Finnish), a largely Swedish-speaking autonomous province of Finland, which has a milder, more maritime, climate than that of the rest of Finland.

Unlike many countries, the same physical characteristics are found all over Finland, and the four geographic regions are differentiated by subtle social and geographical qualities rather than dominant natural features. For instance, in the archipelago rock and water predominate; coastal regions are notable for their clay plains, agriculture and dairy farming; the interior is home to lakes and extensive forests; and upland Finland is home to Arctic scrub. The fish, meat and crops that can be found in these regions feature on regional menus, although many dishes are eaten everywhere.

A climate of extremes

Seasonal variations are dramatic in Finland. Winter is long and dark, with the first snows falling in northern Lapland in October and lasting until April the following year. With such a prolonged cold season, it is no surprise that there is a penchant for warming winter food.

During this time, the lakes and parts of the ocean freeze and even become temporary roads and car parks. But the country copes with winter; trains run, roads stay open and life proceeds as usual. To combat freezing temperatures, which can fall below -30ºC/-22ºF, houses have triple glazing and a good heating system. There is little daylight, but any gloom is offset by reflected light from the snow and bright, clear skies, as well as the astonishingly beautiful spectacle of the aurora, which dances across the sky in resplendent shades of green, blue, red and violet.

Spring is short, but its arrival brings swift and dramatic change. The frozen lakes melt quickly and noisily, filling the rivers and streams to bursting. It is an almost violent change, with the number of daylight hours increasing quickly and the ice and snow being swept away in readiness for the summer's heat.

Left Many Finns own or rent remote summer houses at the edge of lakes.

Summer heralds the arrival of hot weather and extremely short nights – often just twilight when the sun "sets" for a mere hour or so before rising to begin a new day. This glorious season, only occasionally marred by thunderstorms, transforms Finns into an outdoor society. Those living in cities often have access to a summer house in the country. This will be a log cabin on the edge of a lake or on the coast, with a sauna and makeshift barbecue facilities. Ideally, the summer residence will be both difficult to reach and far from neighbours which, in a vast country with a comparatively small population, is achievable. The food changes too in summer, with lake fish, crayfish and large quantities of Finnish beer becoming a regular feature of meals.

The first signs of approaching autumn (which starts in September) are the appearance of wild mushrooms and berries in late August. During this season the days may still be warm but winter's chill creeps up at night.

Wildlife

For those animals that can cope with Finland's tough winter conditions, there is plenty of space to roam freely. Among these hardy beasts are brown bears, wolverines and wolves, who inhabit the wilderness in eastern and northern Finland, and elk, who inhabit the forests and are hunted in season. Reindeer (caribou) can be counted as wild, although they are accompanied by Sami herders.

Above left Positioned between Sweden and Russia, Finland forms a geographical and cultural bridge between east and west.

Above top right With tens of thousands of lakes, rivers and waterways, it is little surprise that fishing is a national hobby.

Above bottom right Brown bears are among the wild animals in the forests of Finland.

The many lakes and rivers contain salmon, pike, perch, zander, vendace, burbot and crayfish, which are making a return to Finnish lakes after a viral disease decimated their numbers 40 years ago. The coastline of the Baltic has low salinity and this affects the fish it supports. Baltic herring, for example, are smaller and less fatty than those found in the North Sea.

Finland: a brief history

A country of contrasts, Finland has a long and fascinating history of conflict and concession, foreign rule and independence, rural idyll and ever-increasing urbanization. In the last 50 years, the country has undergone a dramatic transformation: from an economy and way of life based on farming and forestry to a diversified industrial economy, making modern Finland a global player in the fields of manufacturing, design, sport and music.

Finland marks the northern frontier between east and west Europe, between the Lutheran, formerly Catholic, western Church and the eastern Orthodox Church and, historically, between the Swedish and Russian empires. It is therefore not surprising that many different influences have helped shape every aspect of this individual country.

Mapping the population

There is little written evidence of the early Finns that predates the Roman historian Tacitus. However, just as the topography of the landscape can be traced to a recent ice age, so the origins of the modern population can be traced through its language and, more recently, via DNA testing.

The evidence from these sources points to a people with origins in the Ural Mountains, who made their way west, arriving in Finland from the south and east. It is known that there was also some migration from eastern Sweden, and today many western coastal areas of modern Finland are still predominantly Swedish speaking.

The impact of Christianity

Information about the early history of Finland becomes clearer with the arrival of Christianity, and written records, in the 12th century. During this period, Irish monks converted the pagan Swedes and, through them, their Finnish neighbours. This is thought to have been a relatively peaceful process; the real power struggle, between the conflicting branches of Christianity, came later.

Around 1240, Swedish crusaders, sanctioned by Rome, unsuccessfully attempted to invade Orthodox Russia. There then followed further attacks in 1242 and 1293, followed by a 30-year war between the Swedes and the Russians. This was resolved in 1323, under the treaty of Pähkinäsaari, with Finland being divided between Sweden and Novgorod, the Russian power in the east.

Left A Sami sleigh driver with his reindeer. The Sami were among the worst affected by the period of Swedish rule.

Under the conditions of this treaty, the Russian-held Karelia in the east came under Orthodox rule from Novgorod. The remaining south and west of Finland remained Catholic, becoming part of the Swedish state, with the coastal city of Turku (Åbo in Swedish) as its provincial capital. Catholicism did not survive the Reformation in the 16th century, however, and the entire Swedish state, including its Finnish province, embraced Lutheran Protestantism.

The effects of this split are still evident in the bread that can be found in different regions of Finland. In the west, under the Lutheran and Roman-Catholic influence, bread is traditionally hard, thin and long-lasting, whereas in the east, influenced by the Slavic culture and the Orthodox church, soft loaves made with buttermilk are baked on a daily basis.

Other traces of the Catholic influence, particularly in south-west Finland, are apparent in the food that is served at certain times of the year. For instance, traditional foods, such as pea soup, pancakes and blinis, are eaten on Shrove Tuesday, and mämmi, a rye pudding, is eaten at Easter.

Swedish rule

In the 16th century, Sweden was a major power, controlling not only Scandinavia but also large areas of Germany and eastern European territory. Finns at this time were recruited as soldiers to fight for the Swedes in foreign wars, and heavy taxes, in the form of fur, grain, butter and money were extracted to pay for it all. The Sami hunters, fishermen and small-scale farmers who occupied the northern parts of Finland, came under particular pressure, as the emerging nation states of Swedes, Norwegians and Russians all claimed the right to tax them.

Right A statue of Tsar Alexander II in the Senate Square in front of St Nicholas's Lutheran Cathedral. Many cities have such statues of, and streets named after, him.

During this period, the area of farmed land in Finland grew considerably as, encouraged by the crown, farmers from the province of Savo in the south were urged to relocate to the remote regions in northern and central Finland. Here, they employed traditional slash-and-burn agricultural techniques, often forcing out the indigenous Sami people who inhabited the vast wilderness.

Russian rule

At the beginning of the 18th century, Sweden's power started to wane, while Russia grew ever stronger. The rivalry between these two powerful countries made Finland, positioned between the two, strategically and symbolically important, with Russia wanting to use Finland as a buffer against any foreign aggression towards their homeland.

Lured by such a tempting prize, Russia attacked Finland in 1808, defeating the Swedes and occupying the country. In 1809, Finland signed the Treaty of Fredrikshamn, pledging allegiance to Russia, and became an autonomous Grand Duchy in the Russian Empire. This arrangement with Tsar Alexander I worked well for Finland: the people were allowed to keep their Lutheran faith and any rights gained under Swedish rule, as well as their national identity. Helsinki became the nation's capital.

The succeeding Tsar, Alexander II, was also a popular figure in Finland. Despite ruthless suppression of the Poles and Lithuanians, he had a reputation as an enlightened and liberal ruler. His reforms in Finland led to the establishment of its separate currency, the markka, and the elevation of the Finnish language to a status equal to Swedish. Most cities have a major street called Aleksanterinkatu in honour of this well-loved monarch.

Later Tsars, however, were less well disposed to their Grand Duchy, an attitude that caused Finnish nationalism to gain ground. Ironically, the institutions of state in Finland (its parliament, political freedoms and status as an autonomous region) put in place by the previous Tsars meant that the country was well equipped for independence.

Establishing nationalism

Tensions between Finland and Russia were further heightened following Russian defeats in the Russo-Japanese War of 1904–5. Very high casualty figures and a sense that Russia was being run incompetently resulted in a period of civil unrest throughout the Russian Empire and, in Finland, a feeling that change was needed took hold.

This independent mood was manifested in the introduction of universal suffrage by the Finnish parliament in 1906, making Finland the first European country to grant women the vote.

Russia responded to the call for independence by tightening its grip on its seemingly wayward Grand Duchy, provoking even stronger resistance among the Finns. There then followed a decade of struggle, during which activists, such as Pehr Svinhufvud (who later became the president of Finland), were exiled to Siberia. This lasted until World War I and the Communist revolution brushed aside the Tsars in Russia, making way for a different set of problems for the putative Finnish state.

Finnish independence

On December 6, 1917, Finland declared independence from Russia. A month later, Lenin and the Soviet government granted the new state official recognition.

Sadly, instead of progress and prosperity, a bloody four-month civil war between the Reds (socialists) and the Whites (anti-socialists) erupted, following years of tension over issues such as land reform and democratization.

The war ended in 1918 with victory for the White Army, led by Marshal Carl Gustaf Mannerheim. Mannerheim is a major figure in the shaping of modern independent Finland. With an aristocratic background (as the third son of a count, Mannerheim was a baron), he was a Lieutenant General in the Tsar's army and saw action in the Russo-Japanese war and World War I.

His political opinions did not suit the new Communist government in Soviet Russia, however, and he fell out of favour. Returning to Finland, he headed the White action in Finland's civil war but, urging reconciliation with the losing Red faction, he was dismayed by the actions of the victorious White government, who ruthlessly executed around 8,500 people in areas that had previously been Red.

After years of working to obtain international recognition of Finland's independence, supporting many humanitarian pursuits, and performing various political and military roles, Mannerheim was eventually regarded by both sides as a patriotic and national, rather than factional, leader. Following his death in 1951, he continues to be respected to this day. Indeed, he is one of the few figures to have a dish named after him – Mannerheim vorschmack, a dish of roasted beef, lamb and onions, ground with salted herring and anchovies.

Prohibition

Lasting until 1932, prohibition was introduced in Finland in 1917 as a result of decades of temperance propaganda. At one point, an alcohol ration card was issued to allow only a specific and small daily purchase. There were no pubs or bars, and restaurants were allowed to serve wine or beer only as an accompaniment to food.

As in America, these restrictions spawned a thriving black market and a high level of cunning and subterfuge, resulting in such strange sights as men in restaurants drinking beer beside piles of paid for, but uneaten, sandwiches.

Today, Finns, like Scandinavians in general, have an ambivalent relationship with alcohol, which, until very recently, was governed by a state monopoly, making it not only difficult to obtain, but very expensive.

World War II

A different agenda, centring on the country's relationship with the newly formed Soviet Union, meant that World War II affected Finland differently from other European countries.

The Russians at this time wanted to set up military bases on islands in the Gulf of Finland as part of its protection strategy for nearby Leningrad. This led to protracted but unsuccessful talks between the two nations, followed by a Russian attack on Finland in November 1939. A short, bitter war, with heavy casualties on both sides was fought until, in March 1940, Karelia was ceded to Russia, forcing the Karelians to be evacuated to other parts of Finland. Peace was short-lived, however, and, in June 1940, the Continuation War, Jatko Sota, with Russia began, lasting until 1947, when a peace treaty was eventually signed.

Finland's quarrel with Russia and the Soviet demand for Finland to demobilize most of its armed forces, weakened the country, enabling German troops occupying Norway to cross into Lapland in order to sever Allied supply lines to Leningrad. When the German soldiers retreated southwards they left a line of devastation, burning much of Lapland, including its capital, Rovaniemi, and forcing most of Lapland's inhabitants to be evacuated to Sweden.

Following the signing of the peace treaty in 1947, massive reparations were paid to the Soviet Union and more land was ceded. This forced the economy to undergo radical change and regeneration. A careful political line was needed to maintain peace and, ultimately, it was only with the disintegration of the Soviet Union that Finland was really able to take its proper place in world affairs.

Economic and cultural growth

In the 1960s, relations between Russia and Finland reached a low point when the Soviets tried to interfere in internal Finnish politics. Despite this, the decade heralded the beginning of Finnish economic growth, with the development of ship building, forestry and the paper industry. A significant population shift from rural areas to cities also began. National pride was maintained and, in the following decades, achievements in music, design and sport contributed to this.

Among the important figures are Timo Sarpaneva, Kaj Franck and Tapio Wirkkala, leading international designers who are famous for work with the Iittala glass company. Armi Ratia set up Marimekko, designing fabric and clothing for the likes of Jackie Kennedy. It still sells its distinctive broad stripes, poppies and bold colours. Alvar Aalto worked on building projects from the 1920s until the 1980s, and achieved success with furniture design, lamps and a particular shape of vase, known as "the wave" (aalto in Finnish).

In music, Aulis Sallinen, Einojuhani Rautavaara and Joonas Kokkonen were writing opera, while performers, including Martti Talvela, Kim Borg, Jorma Hynninen and Karita Mattila, performed it.

The country also has a long history of sporting achievement. Hannes Kolehmainen was the first runner to be known as the Flying Finn, taking three gold medals at the 1912 Stockholm Olympics. The nickname passed to Paavo Nurmi, who won three gold medals at the Belgian Olympiad of 1920, and to Lasse Virén, who won the 5,000 metre and 10,000 metre events in both 1972 and 1976. The country also boasts motor-sport successes, having dominated rallying for decades. Famous Formula One drivers include Keke Rosberg, Mika Häkkinen and Kimi Räikkönen.

Finland's biggest company today is Nokia, the world's largest mobile (cell) phone manufacturer. The company originated as a pulp mill next to the Nokia rapids, moving into rubber goods before electronics and mobile phone technology.

Below Paavo Nurmi, the second "Flying Finn", is just one of Finland's sporting heroes.

Below The world-famous soprano Karita Mattila, perfoming in Wagner's *Lohengrin*.

Festivals and holidays

As everywhere, Finnish festivals and holidays provide an opportunity for time out to observe traditional rites, socialize, share meals and have fun. Most of Finland's national holidays are religious in origin, the exceptions being Independence Day (December 6), Midsummer's Day and May Day. Easter, Whitsun and Ascension Day are public holidays. Individuals celebrate their name day with their families and friends, and important birthdays warrant the usual fuss.

Easter (Pääsiäinen)

The Orthodox Church celebrates Easter on a grand scale and, although Finland follows the western church calendar, some Orthodox influences can be seen across the country. These include the lighting of bonfires and, in western Finland, children dressing as witches and going from house to house to collect sweets (candies). Traditional dishes include kulitsa, a yeast pudding that is eaten to mark the end of Lent, and mämmi, a rye flour pudding, flavoured with malt and orange, which is boiled, then creamed and baked in baskets.

May Day (Vappu)

This long-awaited day, on April 30, heralds the beginning of spring, an event that is a cause for a major celebration. Sima and tippaleivat, May Day mead and doughnuts, are usually on offer, along with other alcoholic drinks, such as beer. As with most feast days in Finland, the real celebration happens the evening before, on Walpurgis night, when bonfires are lit, ostensibly to scare off witches, in a similar way to Hallowe'en. These bonfire and witch associations were originally brought from northern Germany to Finland by early settlers, and have now become an integral part of the spring celebration.

Midsummer's Day (Juhannus)

This celebration of the longest day of the year is an occasion for more bonfires and celebrations. Juhannus means "the feast of John the Baptist", an event that is celebrated across many other European countries, with bonfires, singing, dancing and drinking. The connection with the saint is, however, coincidental, and it is the summer solstice that is at the heart of the celebrations in Finland.

Left It is traditional for girls in western Finland to dress up as witches and collect sweets and chocolates from neighbours at Easter.

Held on the Saturday closest to the actual date of the solstice, Juhannus is normally a countryside occasion, with most Finns decamping from cities to find a lake or seaside party. Birch branches and flowers are brought inside to decorate homes, and many people will erect a pole, like a Maypole, with the same pagan fertility associations.

Juhannus is also the Finnish flag day. Flags are raised at six o'clock in the evening on Midsummer's Eve and lowered at nine o'clock the following evening.

Independence Day (Itsenäisyyspäivä)

The day Finland declared independence from Russia is marked on December 6. It is a social, rather than traditional, celebration, and involves processions, flag-waving and grand gatherings at the presidential palace. It is a day for blue and white, Finland's national colours, quiet reflection and the lighting of candles.

Christmas (Joulu) and New Year

A period of cheer during the long months of almost unbroken night, Christmas is a festival of light and warmth in Finland. The main celebration occurs on Christmas Eve: at noon the President declares "Christmas peace" from Turku. Christmas dinner is eaten early in the evening and children are visited by Father Christmas after the meal. It is traditional to light candles and put up

decorations made of straw around the house. The traditional meal includes a baked ham with salads and rice pudding to follow. Christmas Day itself is a quieter and more reflective occasion.

The New Year is marked in much the same way as it is in the rest of the world, with fireworks and general revelry.

Smaller festivals

All Saints' Day (Pyhäinpäivä) at the end of October/start of November, like Christmas Eve, is marked with the lighting of candles, which are then placed on family graves.

Other national days include Runeberg's Day on February 5, which marks the birthday of the popular Swedish poet, Johan Runeberg, when cakes named after him are eaten.

Kalevala day on February 28 is dedicated to the national epic poem, which holds a special place in Finnish culture and history. The Kalevala is a collection of the early myths and folklore surrounding the Finnish people, and was created by Elias Lönnrot in the early 19th century. It plays an important role in the country's sense of separate and unique identity and has influenced music and literature. The poem's metre and style (with running rhythm and alliteration) inspired Henry Longfellow's poem, Hiawatha. Its stories of the earth's creation, of heroes like Ilmarinen (a Finnish sky god) or the sage and magician Väinämöinen, inspired J.R.R.Tolkien's Lord of the Rings.

Valentine's Day, February 14, has become Friendship Day in Finland and is marked by the buying and giving of greeting cards.

Mother's Day is a relatively recent addition to the calendar, having come to Europe from America at the beginning of the 20th century.

Arts festivals

The short summer is the season for world-class festivals. The two most famous are music based – Pori's jazz festival and Savonlinna's opera festival. The former has attracted international

Above left Father Christmas on his rounds with real reindeer on Christmas Eve.

Above Dancers at a Midsummer's Day festival on Seurasaari Island.

stars and the latter plays host to everyone in the opera world, including international Finnish stars.

There are lots of lesser-known events, including an organ festival in Lahti, song festivals in Naantali and Joensuu, and 30 symphony orchestras at work nurturing talented musicians who are now making an impact worldwide. Theatre, poetry and dance festivals are held around the country.

Family celebrations

Rites of passage, such as birthdays and coming of age, are celebrated in Finland much as elsewhere, with cards, presents, parties and favourite foods. Significant birthdays merit more fuss. The person's name day is also celebrated by the giving of cards and presents.

The Finnish cuisine

If there is one theme that summarizes Finnish cooking, it is seasonality. The cuisine is focused on food's integrity rather than the artifice with which it may be prepared, resulting in a repetoire of uncomplicated yet delicious and healthy dishes, which are cooked with care. Other important customs include baking, the coffee table and hospitality.

The food of Finland has its roots in traditional country fare, which makes good use of simple, local ingredients – including root vegetables, wheat, wild and domestic meat, fish, and a wide range of dairy products. Over time, the food has evolved to incorporate haute cuisine and continental-style cooking techniques. Serious health concerns have also brought about a dramatic reduction in the amount of fat and salt used. The result is a diet that is notable for its use of wholegrain products, seasonal fresh berries and vegetables, and meat and fish.

Seasonal cooking

While Finnish supermarkets now offer access to a global larder, the national taste still favours pea soup, rye bread and herring. Market squares (tori) sell a range of fresh, seasonal produce, usually grown or made locally, including such delicacies as wild mushrooms and berries from Lapland.

These open markets are still a popular part of everyday shopping, in spite of the increased number of supermarkets, and Finns still choose to buy home-grown produce because the air freighting of exotic alternatives is an expensive option.

Cooking techniques

The rural traditions that form the basis of the national cusine mean that long, slow-cooking techniques, suitable for a farm oven, are common. This has resulted in a wide range of hearty meat casseroles and hot-pots, which combine the plentiful supplies of venison and pork with root vegetables, such as potatoes, turnips, celeriac and carrots.

Smoking and marinating raw fish are also central to Finnish cuisine, since these procedures infuse the fish with the salty and smoked flavours the Finns love, as well as preserving them.

Mealtime traditions

Breakfast is the main family meal of the day in Finland, and it usually consists of a number of warming, sustaining foods, such as porridge (puuro), which is served with a pat of butter or some fruit or jam; wholegrains such as muesli, bran and other cereals, served with yogurt or fermented soured milk (villi); and open sandwiches, often made with wholemeal (whole-wheat) bread and topped with butter and a variety of savoury foods, such as cheese or cold meats. Coffee is almost always drunk at breakfast, along with milk or buttermilk, although tea is becoming increasingly popular.

Left A wide range of fresh produce is sold at outdoor markets, such as this one in the market square in Helsinki.

Lunch is often a light meal, consisting of a sandwich or a salad, although in schools every pupil is entitled to a free hot meal as part of Finland's welfare state agenda.

Dinner is usually a hot meal, served with a selection of vegetables. Baked vegetable puddings (laatikko), often made from carrots, potato or swede (rutabaga) are a particular Finnish speciality. Desserts are popular, and vary according to what is in season.

The coffee table

Finns traditionally bake very good bread. Dark, flavoursome rye and barley loaves are a major part of the diet, and are often enhanced by cereals, such as oats, that soften the dough and lend complexity to the bread. However, it is the sweet breads, such as pulla, the cardamom-scented, braided sweet bread, and the extravagance of the coffee table offerings that showcase Finnish baking.

Finnish coffee table

Recipes that could be served at a formal coffee table include:
Coffee Bread (Pulla)
Karelian Cheese Tart (Rahkatorttu)
Spice Cake (Pehmeä maustekakku)
Raspberry Jam Biscuits
   (Vadelmapyörykät)

The Finnish coffee table involves more than a few sandwiches, cookies or a piece of cake – it is an important event that marks birthdays, anniversaries, weddings, christenings and funerals. Particularly splendid coffee tables are called for at Christmas and Easter, or to honour a special guest.

The coffee table has its own etiquette, which should be observed by everyone. Tradition dictates that the first visit to the coffee table is reserved for the guest of honour. Coffee bread (pulla) is eaten with the first cup of coffee, followed by a slice of plain cake with the second cup, moving on to more elaborate cakes and biscuits (cookies) with the third cup, and whatever has been missed previously with the fourth, and subsequent, cups.

Above Even on ordinary days, families like to gather to drink coffee and eat pulla.

This may sound like a lot of coffee, but Finns drink coffee in the same way as Germans, making a soft, mild but deep-flavoured drink, rather than the small, wake-up shots of espresso favoured in the warmer regions of Europe and north Africa.

The coffee is made in a kettle from medium-ground, medium-roast, South American beans, with the water and coffee brought to a tremble, rather than a boil, and then left to both settle and brew. The result is a mellow drink that that can be drunk in the quantities required in order to properly complement a table full of cakes, biscuits and various types of sweet bread.

Voileipäpöytä and seisovapöytä

Pöytä translates as "table". Voileipa, literally meaning "buttered bread", denotes a sandwich and the whole word signifies a buffet-style meal of hand-held snacks and open sandwiches.

Seisovapöytä – meaning "standing table" – is a more elaborate affair, more akin to Sweden's smörgåsbord. The cold table may include marinated or smoked fish, such as salmon and herring (rosolli), cheese, breads, salads and pickles. There are also hot dishes partnered by steamed new potatoes and dill, and baked vegetable puddings.

Finally, there is a table of sweet food, similar to the coffee table, with cakes, biscuits (cookies) and, possibly, whipped berry syllabubs and creams.

Below The grand finale to seisovapöytä, a table of rich cakes and desserts.

Finnish fast food

Traditionally, the urban Finn's answer to street food was liha piirakka, a deep-fried pasty containing meat and rice, and nakki, a frankfurter-style sausage brushed with mild mustard and served in a bun.

German-style boiled sausages, makkara, have always been a popular fast food option. These are sold at street stalls at night and in market places during the day. With the recent demand for healthier foods, sausages have undergone a transformation, with the meat content being increased and animal fat being replaced with healthier vegetable fats. Beneficial additives, such as nutritious pine bark flour, are also being added.

As a result of the changes, sausages are more popular than ever, and the visit to the sauna, which is still a major part of

Above left Sausages are eaten everywhere in Finland, and make a convenient meal cooked over a wood fire on a hunting trip.

Above Karelian rye pastries make a delicious and handy snack and are enjoyed all over Finland.

Finnish social culture, would be deemed incomplete without a sauna makkara – sauna sausage ring – which is cooked on the stones that heat the sauna and is eaten when the bathers have finished.

Finnish ice cream is sold in the street kiosks and market places and is a sure harbinger of spring. Like most dairy products in Finland, the quality of ice cream on offer has always been high and even the mass-produced versions contain good ingredients. Perhaps for this reason, Finland's annual ice cream consumption is the highest in Europe.

Regional food

Although many dishes can be found throughout Finland, there are a number of notable regional specialities. These include kalakukko, a fish and pork pie wrapped in a rye crust, which is the most famous dish from the Savo region in eastern Finland. Although it is found elsewhere, the market square in Kuopio, a city in northern Savo, claims to be the first, and still the best, place to buy ready-made kalakukko.

Lapland is famous for its rich, hearty stews, often made with venison, such as reindeer (caribou) and elk; berries, such as the arctic cloudberry; and salmon, which is often smoked or dried to preserve it and add flavour. Hunting, fishing and gathering wild foods are still at the core of the diet in Lapland, and determine what is eaten on a daily basis.

Karelian food derives its style from Russia, rather than Scandinavia, and includes Karelian stews, (karjalanpaisti), slow-cooked hotpots, in which any meat will work well. Moccasin-shaped rye pasties (karjalanpiirakat) are also popular. These handy snacks have a rice filling and are often served with chopped hard-boiled egg and butter. Easy to transport, sustaining and delicious, they are the most famous dish from the region and are made and bought all over the country.

With seasonality and availability at the heart of Finnish cooking, it is little surprise that sea fish – such as lampreys in Pori, a city on the west coast, and smoked Baltic sprats and herrings elsewhere – feature on menus at eateries along the shoreline and on the islands that comprise the archipelago, while freshwater fish, such as pike, perch and trout, dominate in lakeside restaurants farther inland.

The restaurant scene

Restaurant dining is a relatively recent phenomenon in Finland. In times past restaurants were primarily places to dance or drink. This has changed dramatically in recent years, and is slowly having an impact on the Finnish food scene as a whole.

The capital, Helsinki, is at the heart of the restaurant revolution, with a growing number of Finnish chefs creating exciting new dishes from the country's traditional ingredients. However, this new generation of successful Finns is looking for more than the classic slow-cooked stews and root vegetable bakes, and this has spawned some interesting adaptations that draw their inspiration from haute cuisine, such as reindeer steaks with chanterelle mushroom stuffing, perch consommé with crayfish ravioli and herring parfait.

Above left Whole fillets of salmon, pegged to a board and cooked over a wood fire, are called loimutettu lohi, "blazed" salmon.

Above Arctic cloudberries are among the many wild berries picked in Lapland and sold at markets all over the country.

Dill and wild berries are still used to finish the dishes, adding the final Finnish touch to the fusion dishes, and displaying their new-found confidence.

A similar change can be seen in the nation's attitude to wine, which is now regularly drunk with meals. In the past, it could only legally be bought from the state Alko shops. It was costly and the choice was limited, so people drank beer or spirits instead. The arrival of wine has not, however, brought about the demise of the Finnish beer industry. Instead, it has heightened the dining experience.

Finnish ingredients

With its vast, open spaces, coniferous forests and freshwater lakes, Finland is home to a range of wild and domestic animals, freshwater fish, hardy winter vegetables and a glorious glut of wild and cultivated berries during the brief, but productive, summer. As a result of the challenging climate, Finnish cuisine is designed to counteract the long winter, with warming, hearty meat stews and satisfying soups dominating the menu. There is also a wealth of summer dishes that make full use of fresh fruit and vegetables, providing a year-round feast for the stomach.

Many of the ingredients commonly used in Finland, such as pork, lamb and beef, and root vegetables, are familiar all over the world. In addition to these basics, however, there are some Finnish ingredients that may be more difficult to find outside Scandinavia. Alternative suggestions are offered in the recipes, making the dishes more accessible.

Some familiar ingredients are more widely used in Finnish cooking than elsewhere. For example, dill is the favourite herb and it garnishes most dishes, especially potatoes. It is fresh and fragrant, with the slightest hint of aniseed, far less pronounced in flavour than fennel leaves, which look very similar but taste quite different.

Domestic and wild meat

The extreme climate in Finland makes animal husbandry more difficult than in a temperate climate. Livestock needs to be sheltered from the cold in barns throughout most of the winter, before being allowed to graze outdoors for the brief, but glorious, summer.

Pork is the mainstay of many Finnish meals, particularly in the south and west of the country. At one time, every farmhouse kept a couple of pigs to eat the household scraps. Practical and versatile, the entire pork carcass was used, with fresh cuts, sausages, preserved hams and many different charcuterie items made from the odds and ends; even the blood was made

into pancakes that were served with some sharp wild berries. Traditionally, a pork chop was served with a mound of crayfish tails and some dill in late summer, then, in winter, ham was the centrepiece of Finland's Christmas feast. Such strong culinary traditions endure, even when the meat is not from the household's own pig.

Finland has a large dairy-farming sector and beef has always played an important part in the national diet. Traditional slow-cooking techniques suit the meat perfectly. It is also frequently minced (ground) and used to make

Below, left to right: Pig's trotters; pork fillet; reindeer meat.

meatballs or a meat sauce, mixed with root vegetables, such as potato, to make pies and pasties, or served almost raw as steak tartare.

Until recently, lamb was rarely on offer, except at Easter when it is traditionally served roasted. Today, however, it is as popular as any other meat and often features in stews and casseroles. It is also ground and used to stuff cabbage leaves, or smoked.

When it comes to wild meat, including elk, reindeer (caribou in North America), hare and game birds, Finns are spoilt for choice. Elk (moose in North America) are big beasts that roam large parts of Finland, including the southern regions, and can pose a threat to motorists in winter.

The elk-hunting season begins in late September, so those with a hunting permit are able to shoot their own dinner. It is Finland's most widely hunted animal; approximately 87,000 are shot each season. The carcasses produce large joints of dark, well-flavoured red meat. Both heart and liver can also be eaten.

Reindeer have dark meat, similar to beef, but less fatty and gelatinous than that of elk. In Finland, all the offal from reindeer is used as well as its meat, so reindeer liver and reindeer tongue recipes are popular. The meat from these animals is routinely smoked and sold as charcuterie – delicious with new potatoes and salad.

In addition to the larger beasts, hares and game birds are widely eaten, both stewed or roasted. Bear meat is also available, but this remains more of a curiosity than a traditional dish.

Fish

With two gulfs, the Baltic Sea, hundreds of rivers and tens of thousands of lakes in Finland, it is little wonder that catching and consuming fish is a national passion. Common ways of preparing the fish include salting, hot- and cold-smoking, and baking in paper. Pies, pasties, chowders and stews are also popular.

The majority of the waterways are freshwater, and the Baltic is more like a large lake in terms of salt levels compared to other seas. Baltic fish tend to be slightly different from those found elsewhere, and some of the traditional recipes in this book may require carefully chosen alternatives.

Above, left to right: Perch; fresh salmon; Baltic herrings.

The most popular varieties of fish are vendace, burbot, pike and perch, as well as salmon. Vendace, or muikku, are small fish, the size of anchovies or small sardines. They are generally eaten whole, eyes and bones included.

Burbot is quite similar to monkfish, although monkfish has a more pronounced flavour and slightly firmer flesh. Finnish burbot live at the bottom of lakes and are prized as much for their exquisite livers and roe as their succulent white flesh.

Pike and perch are dry-fleshed fish. Carp is a good alternative, if you can get it; otherwise, a firm-fleshed fish, such as hake, can be used. Pike-perch, a member of the perch family, is also known as zander (or "sandre" in French) and this can be used as a substitute for perch.

Farmed and wild salmon are among the most readily available fish in Finland, and are used in a great many recipes, including soups, pies, bakes and to make gravlax.

Fruit

The wild berries of Finland, as elsewhere, are one of the most spectacular food resources, and there are a large number of recipes for these treasured fruits. Many of the berries, like strawberries and raspberries, are widely available, while others, such as lingonberries and Arctic cloudberries, may be harder to find outside Finland.

As well as the soft berries, rowan berries, buckthorn, juniper berries, rose hips and arctic bramble are also used to flavour stews, or are preserved in jams and jellies. Lingonberries grow in dark, peaty forest areas from July to October. They are very high in pectin and contain good levels of citric acid, which protects them from mould and rot. This means they keep well, even without the addition of sugar, and they make excellent jams, jellies and a delicious after-dinner liqueur. Cranberries are a good substitute and, like lingonberries, the natural sharpness is used in a relish to complement rich meats, such as elk and deer.

Bilberries (wild blueberries) are common on moorland or in high, wild places. They are smaller than cultivated blueberries, and have a more concentrated flavour (in the same way that wild strawberries are more intense than the cultivated varieties). Sweet and delicious, they provide the perfect excuse for a late-summer foraging expedition. Cultivated blueberries can be used instead.

European wild cranberries are slightly smaller than their North American cousins and in Finland they are found in boggy marshlands. When ripe, the berries are red and juicy. They taste quite sharp, but this tartness diminishes after the first frost, so they are often gathered in late autumn.

Arctic cloudberries grow in much of Finland but are most abundant in Lapland. They are yellow-orange in colour, with the appearance and texture of raspberries, but with seeds on the inside rather than the outside of the fruit. They are available only in July and August. Cloudberry jam is available in specialist stores and it is a good alternative to fresh berries in mousses and sweet sauces. Lakka is a sweet liqueur made from cloudberries, and this can also be used in desserts that call for the berries.

Above, left to right Strawberries; cultivated blueberries; canned cloudberries and lakka, the sweet cloudberry liqueur.

Vegetables

The severe climate limits the range of vegetables that can be successfully grown in Finland. Root vegetables are, perhaps unsurprisingly, the common staples. They are stored in barns for winter and feature in many traditional recipes, including stews, mashes and slow-cooked dishes. Among the types on offer are swede (rutabaga), carrots, parsnips, celeriac, beetroot (beet) and, of course, potatoes.

Potatoes, especially the waxy varieties of the spring new crop, are the national favourite. Lapin puikula, yellow Finn potatoes, come from Lapland and are dug in the autumn. These small, long and curved potatoes have a floury texture and yellow flesh, and are the traditional accompaniment to Sami reindeer (caribou) stews. They have been given special protection by European Union regulations (in much the same way as Camembert and Parma ham has in France and Italy).

Dairy produce

Finland offers some of the best dairy produce in the world in terms of quality, purity and taste. This is partly because additives or hormones are not permitted in cattle rearing or milk production, resulting in a very high-quality product.

Finns have always drunk plenty of milk and it is common to see people drink a pint with their meal. There are many different types of milk available, including skimmed, semi-skimmed (low-fat) and full-fat (whole) milk, as well as buttermilk and curd milk (viili). Beesting milk, the rich, creamy milk produced by a cow after calving, is used to make a delicious pudding called uunijuusto.

There are also several buttermilk products, including piima, a popular light, sharp, refreshing and low-fat buttermilk drink, and kefir, a rich, pourable drink made from fermented buttermilk.

Cream products include smetana, a high-fat, sour-tasting cream that is made by curdling milk and that has its origins in Russia; crème fraîche; clotted buffalo cream; and a curd cream, kermaviili. Cream cheeses are used for making desserts such as Karelian Cheese Tart.

The thriving cheese-making industry in Finland has been making excellent cheese since the 13th century. These include juustoleipa, an unusual baked cheese originally made from reindeer milk in northern Finland, and lappi, a semi-soft cheese from Lapland that is used in recipes and for melting. Turunmaa is another semi-soft cheese, with a mild and creamy flavour that makes it an ideal breakfast cheese. Finlandia Swiss is a sharp, rindless cheese, similar to Swiss Emmenthal. Its strength is denoted by the colour of the label, blue being the mildest, red being medium-strength, and black being a strong mature cheese.

Groceries

Although the majority of store-cupboard items are similar to those used elsewhere, there are a few variations. Potato flour, for instance, is preferred to cornflour (cornstarch) for thickening sauces, and Finnish mustards tend to be quite sweet and mild, rather like the German and Swedish varieties, and are made from a combination of white and brown mustard seeds. The sugar is made from home-grown beet, rather than imported cane.

Alcohol

All alcoholic drink is expensive in Finland and there are still traces of historic restrictions from the prohibition era. Beer and wine are now on sale in supermarkets, but anything stronger is still part of a state monopoly. Entry into the European Union has had an impact on the sale of alcohol, however, especially as Estonia (also an EU member) is just a short boat ride away, and sells alcohol far more cheaply. As a result of this competition, prices are slowly beginning to drop in Finland.

Finnish beer is of the Pilsner lager type. The most popular brands are Lapin Kulta (literally Lapland gold), Lahden olut (beer from Lahti) and Karjala (literally Karelia). The beers come in different strengths, as in Russia: the strengths range from "I" (almost no alcohol content) to "IV" (high alcohol content), though oddly "II" is missing from the list.

The national spirit is Koskenkorva, a fiery, vodka-like drink, although Finlandia vodka and Jaloviina are also popular.

Below, left to right: Clotted buffalo cream; Finnish mustard; potato flour.

Appetizers & side dishes

Hearty soups & vegetable bakes

Appetizers as a separate first course are not a major feature of Finnish mealtimes. Soups tend to be robust and need only the addition of some bread and cheese or ham for them to be a complete, sustaining meal. Important occasions will, however, see a selection of salads served as hors d'oeuvres. This system is much the same as that used by Finland's immediate neighbours; Swedes offer smörgåsbord – voileipäpöytä in Finnish – and Russians, zakouski.

The main difference between dishes offered as appetizers and those kept for main courses is that an appetizer should stimulate the palate rather than satisfy the belly. Highly flavoured food is best eaten in smaller quantities, leaving room for, perhaps, a hearty meat or fish dish partnered by comforting carbohydrates like potato or bread at the next stage of the meal.

Vegetables are not automatic accompaniments to the main course in Finland, and many dishes incorporate vegetables such as beetroot (beet) or celeriac as part of the recipe, negating the need for additional side dishes.

When summer vegetables arrive, however, they are celebrated. Dishes like kesakeitto have evolved as a showcase for all the fragile delicacy of the new season, flaunting the delicious taste of baby carrots and potatoes, peas and spinach without the need for spices or the strong flavours of herbs and wine. To recreate this sort of dish best, the vegetables should be just lifted and still sweet. It is well worth checking each bunch of carrots for crispness and scraping away a section of a potato's skin, which will come away effortlessly if it has been recently dug.

Serves 4

50g/2oz/¼ cup unsalted (sweet) butter

1 leek, white part only, chopped

1 shallot, chopped

250g/9oz ceps, thickly sliced

25g/1oz/¼ cup plain (all-purpose) flour

1 litre/1¾ pints/4 cups light chicken stock (see below)

100ml/3½oz/scant ½ cup double (heavy) cream

15ml/1 tbsp chopped fresh parsley

salt and ground black pepper

For the stock

500g/1¼lb chicken wings

1 small onion, chopped

1 leek, green part only, chopped

1.5 litres/2½ pints/6¼ cups water

Cook's tip To clean the ceps, use a small, sharp knife to scrape any soil or leaf away from the stalk, then clean the caps with a pastry brush. If they really need washing, then do so just before cooking and pat the mushrooms dry as soon as they are clean.

Cep mushroom soup
Herkkutattikeitto

Italy is not the only country besotted with these mushrooms, called porcini in Italian, cèpe in French and penny bun or cep in English. They grow mainly in southern and central parts of Finland, where they are called herkkutatti. Extremely versatile and with a wonderful nutty flavour, they are deservedly the most sought-after fungus after truffles.

1 To make the stock, preheat the oven to 200°C/400°F/Gas 6. Put the chicken wings, onion and leek in a roasting pan and roast in the oven for about 25 minutes until golden brown. Discard any residual fat in the pan and pour in 350ml/12fl oz/1½ cups of the water. Place the pan on top of the stove and bring the liquid to the boil, stirring all the time to incorporate the residue on the bottom of the pan.

2 Transfer both the chicken and pan juices to a clean pan. Top up with the remaining water and add the vegetables. Bring to the boil then reduce the heat and simmer for 40 minutes to 1 hour. Strain the juices into a jug (pitcher). (This should yield about 1 litre/1¾ pints/4 cups stock.)

3 To make the soup, heat the butter in a large pan, add the leek, shallot and mushrooms and fry until beginning to soften. Stir in the flour and cook over a low heat for 30 seconds. Add about a third of the stock and, stirring all the time, bring to the boil. Reduce the heat and simmer for 3–4 minutes, then add the remaining stock. Season the soup to taste with salt and pepper.

4 Stir the cream and chopped parsley into the soup and heat gently. Pour into individual serving bowls and serve hot.

Per portion Energy 262kcal/1081kJ; Protein 3.1g; Carbohydrate 7.8g, of which sugars 2.2g; Fat 24.5g, of which saturates 15g; Cholesterol 61mg; Calcium 46mg; Fibre 1.8g; Sodium 291mg.

50g/2oz/¼ cup unsalted (sweet) butter

50g/2oz/1 cup plain (all-purpose) flour

700ml/1 pint 3½fl oz/scant 3 cups fish or chicken stock

5ml/1 tsp paprika

1 egg yolk

120ml/4fl oz/½ cup double (heavy) cream

250g/9oz cooked crayfish meat

15ml/1 tbsp lemon juice

salt and ground black pepper

15ml/1 tbsp chopped fresh dill, to garnish

Crayfish soup
Rapukeitto

Crayfish are delicate and delicious and the sweetness of the meat gives a distinctive taste to the creamy soup. Paprika and lemon juice contrast well with the crayfish, and the remaining ingredients highlight the flavour of the shellfish rather than competing with or disguising it.

1 Melt the butter in a pan, stir in the flour to make a roux and cook over a low heat for 30 seconds, without colouring. Remove from the heat and gradually stir in the fish or chicken stock to form a smooth sauce.

2 Return the pan to the heat and, stirring all the time, cook until the sauce boils and thickens. Add the paprika and season to taste with salt and pepper.

3 In a small bowl, mix the egg yolk and cream together, then stir into the soup and heat gently, taking care not to let the mixture boil or the soup will curdle.

4 Add the crayfish and lemon juice to the soup and heat gently. Pour the soup into individual serving bowls and serve hot, garnished with chopped dill.

Per portion Energy 348kcal/1444kJ; Protein 12.2g; Carbohydrate 10.9g, of which sugars 0.8g; Fat 28.8g, of which saturates 17g; Cholesterol 184mg; Calcium 65mg; Fibre 0.4g; Sodium 383mg.

Rustic pea soup with a pig's trotter
Hernekeitto

Flavoursome and warming, this pea soup is a good defence against the cold. With a chunk of bread it makes a fine lunch. The use of a pig's trotter demonstrates the Finn's thriftiness, ensuring that no part of the animal goes to waste, and it also adds a richness to the finished dish.

1 Soak the peas overnight in plenty of cold water. The next day, rinse and put the peas in a pan with the water, pig's trotter, bacon, onion, carrot, leek and allspice.

2 Bring the liquid to the boil. Skim away any foam that rises, then lower the heat, cover and simmer for about 2 hours, until the meat and vegetables are tender. If the soup has thickened too much to your taste, dilute it with a little extra water.

3 Lift out the trotter and cut away the meat, discarding the bones and gristle. Return the meat to the soup and add the dried marjoram and mustard. Taste for seasoning and add salt if needed. Pour into individual serving bowls and serve hot.

Per portion Energy 306kcal/1287kJ; Protein 26.8g; Carbohydrate 27.3g, of which sugars 2.8g; Fat 10.7g, of which saturates 3.6g; Cholesterol 42mg; Calcium 57mg; Fibre 5.7g; Sodium 869mg.

Serves 4

200g/7oz dried peas

1.5 litres/2½ pints/6¼ cups water

1 pig's trotter, split lengthways

200g/7oz smoked bacon, diced

1 onion, chopped

1 carrot, chopped

1 leek, chopped

2.5ml/½ tsp ground allspice

2.5ml/½ tsp dried marjoram

30ml/2 tbsp Swedish, German or Dijon mustard

salt and ground black pepper

Hasselback potatoes
Hasselbackan perunat

This dish is named after the Stockholm restaurant that created it, and is a method of cooking rather than a recipe. Choose similar-sized potatoes so that they cook uniformly, and the essential thing is to cut the potatoes most of the way, but not completely, through. It is a good idea to thread a skewer through the potato three-quarters of the way down before cutting, so that your knife travels just to the point you want it to reach and no farther.

1 Preheat the oven to 200°C/400°F/Gas 6. Peel the potatoes then – and this is the crucial part – cut them widthways, not lengthways, down to three-quarters of their depth at 3mm/⅛in intervals, preferably at a slight angle.

2 Wash the potatoes in cold water then arrange, cut sides uppermost, in a deep, ovenproof dish. Melt the butter, then add the olive oil and mix together. Brush the mixture over the potatoes, then season well with salt and pepper. Sprinkle over the breadcrumbs and cheese.

3 Roast the potatoes in the oven for about 1 hour, depending on their size, until golden brown and fanned apart along the cut lines. Serve hot.

Per portion Energy 380kcal/1593kJ; Protein 9.9g; Carbohydrate 42g, of which sugars 3.1g; Fat 20.4g, of which saturates 12.5g; Cholesterol 52mg; Calcium 182mg; Fibre 2.3g; Sodium 367mg.

Serves 4

4 large potatoes

75g/3oz/6 tbsp butter

45ml/3 tbsp olive oil

50g/2oz/1 cup fine fresh breadcrumbs

50g/2oz/⅔ cup grated Parmesan cheese

salt and ground black pepper

Cook's tip If the potatoes are to be served with a roast joint of meat, use the cooking juices to baste them during cooking. Don't move them around while they roast.

Serves 4

a small knob (pat) of butter

2 eggs

250ml/8fl oz/1 cup full-fat (whole) milk

30ml/2 tbsp plain (all-purpose) flour

5ml/1 tsp salt

2 potatoes

15ml/1 tbsp chopped fresh parsley,
to garnish (optional)

Variation To make a richer, creamier version, substitute half the milk with single (light) cream.

Grated potato casserole
Riivinkropsu

This recipe comes from Satakunta, a south-western region of Finland. Floury, maincrop potatoes will produce the best results.

1 Preheat the oven to 180°C/350°F/Gas 4. Melt the butter and use to grease an ovenproof dish. Beat the eggs together in a bowl then add the milk and mix together. Add the flour and salt and mix to form a batter.

2 Peel the potatoes, then grate them and add to the batter. Transfer the potato mixture to the prepared dish, then bake in the oven for about 50 minutes, until the potatoes are cooked. Serve hot, sprinkled with chopped parsley, if using.

Per portion Energy 215kcal/894kJ; Protein 8.7g; Carbohydrate 13g, of which sugars 3.3g; Fat 14.7g, of which saturates 7.7g; Cholesterol 123mg; Calcium 277mg; Fibre 3g; Sodium 297mg.

Sauerkraut pie
Hapankaalipiiras

Traditionally made with a thin crust of yeast or puff pastry, this delicious pie can be eaten on its own or as an accompaniment to roasted meat. This version uses shortcrust pastry, and is filled with a mixture of sauerkraut, two types of cabbage and chunks of ham. Sauerkraut is sometimes sold canned or in jars with white wine vinegar, and this type can be used without any preparation. However, it is traditionally sold in its fermented state and this needs to be lifted from its brine and washed in warm water to remove any excess saltiness.

1 To make the pastry, put the flour and salt in a large bowl. Cut the butter into small pieces, add to the flour and rub in until the mixture resembles fine breadcrumbs. Alternatively, put the flour and salt in a food processor, add the butter and, using a pulsing action, blend to form fine breadcrumbs. Add the oil and water and mix to form a dough. Shape into a ball, cover with a clean dish towel, then leave to rest in the refrigerator for 1 hour.

2 Rinse the sauerkraut in cold running water if necessary, then put in a pan with the butter and sugar and heat for 1–2 minutes. Add the wine, cover the pan, bring the mixture to the boil, then remove from the heat.

3 Cook the shredded white and the Savoy cabbage in boiling salted water for about 5 minutes until tender, then drain, refresh under cold running water, and drain again. Put in a bowl and add the sauerkraut and ham. Mix together well and transfer to a deep, ovenproof pie dish.

4 Preheat the oven to 180°C/350°F/Gas 4. Roll out the pastry on a lightly floured surface so that it is large enough to cover the dish, and place it over the dish. Combine the egg yolk and water and brush over the pie to glaze. Bake in the oven for 20 minutes or until the pastry is golden brown. Serve hot.

Serves 4

300g/11oz sauerkraut

20g/¾oz/1½ tbsp butter

5ml/1 tsp sugar

100ml/3½fl oz/scant ½ cup white wine

150g/5oz white cabbage, shredded

150g/5oz Savoy cabbage, shredded

150g/5oz boiled ham, cubed

1 egg yolk

5ml/1 tsp water

For the pastry

275g/10oz/2½ cups plain (all-purpose) flour

5ml/1 tsp salt

150g/5oz/10 tbsp unsalted (sweet) butter

45ml/3 tbsp vegetable oil

25ml/1½ tbsp water

Variation To make the dish more substantial, replace the ham with some meatballs.

Per portion Energy 728kcal/3032kJ; Protein 16.3g; Carbohydrate 59.8g, of which sugars 7.4g; Fat 46.8g, of which saturates 24.1g; Cholesterol 163mg; Calcium 190mg; Fibre 5.4g; Sodium 1652mg.

Serves 4

2 eggs

100ml/3½fl oz/scant ½ cup milk

50g/2oz/½ cup plain (all-purpose) flour

5ml/1 tsp baking powder

50g/2oz/4 tbsp butter

500g/1¼lb fresh or frozen spinach

1.5ml/¼ tsp grated nutmeg

salt and ground black pepper

grated Parmesan cheese,
to garnish

Cook's tip After spreading the cooked pancake with the spinach, lift the edges of one of the longer sides and fold a third over the spinach. Lift the edges of the opposite side and then fold this across and over.

Spinach pancake
Pinaattipannukakku

This pancake is made in the oven, then rolled up like a Swiss roll. Grated cheese, such as Parmesan, works well as a garnish.

1 Preheat the oven to 180°C/350°F/Gas 4. Beat the eggs and milk together in a bowl. Sift the flour, 5ml/1 tsp salt and the baking powder into a large bowl, then add the egg mixture and mix together until smooth. Leave to stand for 30 minutes.

2 Cut a piece of baking parchment so that it is slightly bigger than a 25cm x 35cm/ 10in x 14in Swiss (jelly) roll tin (pan), and position in the tin. Melt 15g/½oz/1 tbsp of the butter and brush all over the baking parchment. Pour the batter into the tin and spread it as evenly as you can. Bake in the oven for about 20 minutes, until set.

3 Meanwhile, cook the spinach in only the water clinging to its leaves after washing, for 5–10 minutes, until wilted, or until thawed if using frozen spinach. Drain well and squeeze out as much water as possible. Melt the remaining butter in a pan, then add to the spinach with the nutmeg. Mix together and season with salt and pepper.

4 Chop the spinach slightly then spread across the baked pancake. Roll the pancake up like a Swiss roll and cut into thick slices before serving.

Per portion Energy 215kcal/894kJ; Protein 8.7g; Carbohydrate 13g, of which sugars 3.3g; Fat 14.7g, of which saturates 7.7g; Cholesterol 123mg; Calcium 277mg; Fibre 3g; Sodium 297mg.

Swede pudding
Lanttulaatikko

A traditional Finnish Christmas dish, this baked pudding combines mashed swede with butter and cream to make a delicious vegetable accompaniment. The texture of swede is quite dense compared, for example, with parsnip, so you will need to cut it into relatively small dice or allow for extra cooking time.

1 Put the diced swede in a large pan and cover generously with water. Bring to the boil, lower the heat and simmer for about 20 minutes until tender. Remove the pan from the heat and leave the swede to cool in the water for about 30 minutes. Drain well and mash the swede.

2 Preheat the oven to 180°C/350°F/Gas 4. Grease a deep, ovenproof dish with butter. Pour the cream into a bowl, add the breadcrumbs, nutmeg and salt and mix together. Add the beaten eggs.

3 Add the cream mixture to the mashed swede and mix together. Spoon the mixture into the prepared dish and dot the surface with the butter. Bake in the oven for about 30 minutes until lightly browned. Serve hot.

Per portion Energy 434kcal/1794kJ; Protein 6.3g; Carbohydrate 16.9g, of which sugars 7.4g; Fat 38.5g, of which saturates 22.7g; Cholesterol 185mg; Calcium 123mg; Fibre 2.7g; Sodium 712mg.

Serves 4

1 large swede (rutabaga), diced

40g/1½oz/3 tbsp butter, plus extra for greasing

200ml/7fl oz/scant 1 cup double (heavy) cream

50g/2oz/1 cup fine fresh breadcrumbs

2.5ml/½ tsp grated nutmeg

5ml/1 tsp salt

2 eggs, beaten

Cook's tip Swede (rutabaga), unlike potato, contains no gluten, so it will not turn sticky if puréed in a food processor. The other ingredients can then be added to the processing bowl as soon as the swede is blended.

Carrot bake
Porkkanalaatikko

Carrots and rice are surprisingly well-suited partners. Finns tend to use short grain pudding rice rather than patna or basmati. The characteristic stickiness binds all the other ingredients together to make a satisfying dish.

1 Put the carrots in a large pan and cover generously with water. Bring the water to the boil, lower the heat and simmer for about 20 minutes until the carrots are tender. Remove the carrots with a slotted spoon and mash in a clean pan.

2 Bring the liquid the carrots were cooked in to the boil, then add the salt and the rice and simmer for 25 minutes. Add the milk and simmer until it has been absorbed.

3 Preheat the oven to 200°C/400°F/Gas 6. Use the butter to grease a deep, ovenproof dish. Transfer the cooked rice to a bowl. Add the mashed carrots, sugar and eggs and mix together. Season the mixture with salt and the white pepper.

4 Spoon the carrot mixture into the prepared dish and sprinkle the breadcrumbs over the top. Bake in the oven for 40 minutes until golden brown. Serve hot.

Per portion Energy 280kcal/1171kJ; Protein 7.4g; Carbohydrate 43.7g, of which sugars 18.5g; Fat 9g, of which saturates 4.4g; Cholesterol 110mg; Calcium 94mg; Fibre 3.2g; Sodium 654mg.

Serves 4

500g/1¼lb carrots, sliced

500ml/17fl oz/generous 2 cups water

5ml/1 tsp salt

100g/3¾oz/½ cup short grain rice

100ml/3½fl oz/scant ½ cup milk

25g/1oz/2 tbsp butter, softened, for greasing

30ml/2 tbsp demerara (raw) sugar

2 eggs, beaten

2.5ml/½ tsp ground white pepper

25g/1oz/½ cup fine fresh breadcrumbs

Cook's tip Finns usually start cooking rice for a savoury dish in water as this speeds up the cooking time. Milk can then be added halfway through the cooking to give a creamier texture to the finished dish.

2 cooked beetroots (beets)

1 egg, beaten

100g/3¾oz/2 cups fine fresh breadcrumbs

vegetable oil, for shallow frying

salt and ground black pepper

Beetroot patties
Punajuuripihvit

In the days before air-freighted vegetables, beetroot was a staple ingredient in Finland, and was the basis for a wide variety of imaginative recipes. These delicious patties can be served with a dollop of sour cream as an appetizer or alongside grilled meat or fish to provide a different texture and flavour. They are also often served in conjunction with fried onions.

1 Peel the outer skin from the cooked beetroot using a sharp knife, then cut the flesh into 1cm/½in slices.

2 Break the egg on a plate and beat lightly. Spread the breadcrumbs on a separate plate and season with salt and pepper. Dip the beetroot slices in the egg and then the breadcrumbs, to coat both sides.

3 Heat the oil in a large frying pan, add the coated beetroot and fry for about 5 minutes, turning once, until golden brown on both sides. Drain on kitchen paper and serve hot.

Per portion Energy 174kcal/734kJ; Protein 5.3g; Carbohydrate 23.2g, of which sugars 4.2g; Fat 7.4g, of which saturates 1g; Cholesterol 48mg; Calcium 50mg; Fibre 1.5g; Sodium 241mg.

2 cucumbers

15ml/1 tbsp salt

20ml/2 tbsp white wine vinegar

20ml/2 tbsp caster (superfine) sugar

5ml/1 tsp ground black pepper

sour cream, to serve

Finnish cucumber salad in sweet-and-sour dressing
Kurkkusalaatti

This cucumber salad is made in two parts. First, the cucumber is salted and pressed to extract its juices and then it is squeezed to produce a different textured salad, which is dressed in a sweet-and-sour sugar and vinegar mixture. With a dollop of sour cream it makes a refreshing appetizer, and as a side dish it will cut through any fattiness or richness in stews or braised dishes.

1 Peel and thinly slice the cucumber. Place in a large bowl and sprinkle with the salt. Place a smaller bowl on top and add a heavy weight, such as a can or a full jam jar. Leave to press for 1 hour.

2 Mix the vinegar, sugar and pepper together in a bowl. Taste to check that the balance of sharpness to sweetness is good and adjust if necessary.

3 Lift out the salted cucumber, a handful at a time, and squeeze out as much liquid and salt as possible. Toss in the vinegar and sugar mixture and transfer to a serving dish. Serve with a spoonful of sour cream on top.

Per portion Energy 27kcal/114kJ; Protein 0.6g; Carbohydrate 6.4g, of which sugars 6.3g; Fat 0.1g, of which saturates 0g; Cholesterol 0mg; Calcium 16mg; Fibre 0.5g; Sodium 494mg.

Cook's tip Cucumber loses volume when it is prepared in this way, so allow at least half a cucumber per person.

Honey and sour cream gherkins
Venäläiset kurkut

This salad has Russian origins, and it is traditionally served with a selection of hors d'oeuvres, called zakouski. A shot of vodka would be an appropriate accompaniment, but the salad could also act as a foil to grilled or roast pork.

1 Slice the gherkins lengthways into quarters. Whisk the sour cream until light and foamy, then spoon on to four individual serving plates.

2 Put the butter in a frying pan and heat until melted. Add the gherkin slices and turn in the butter until warmed, then pile on top of the sour cream.

3 Add the honey to the pan and stir until all the butter and residue on the bottom of the pan are incorporated. Spoon over the gherkins and serve hot.

Per portion Energy 106kcal/441kJ; Protein 0.8g; Carbohydrate 12.6g, of which sugars 12.6g; Fat 6.1g, of which saturates 3.8g; Cholesterol 17mg; Calcium 22mg; Fibre 0.2g; Sodium 32mg.

Serves 4

4 large pickled gherkins

60ml/4 tbsp sour cream

15g/½oz/1 tbsp butter

60ml/4 tbsp clear honey

Cook's tip Many varieties of pickled gherkin are available in Scandinavian stores, but it is important to check you don't buy Russian ones by mistake, as they are different from the Finnish ones.

Summer salad with Finnish salad cream dressing

Kesäsalaatti ja kermainen kastike

Mayonnaise and vinaigrette are not the only dressings for a summer salad. Homemade salad cream, such as the one in this recipe, makes a delicious alternative, and tastes much better than store-bought versions.

1 Cut the hard-boiled eggs in half, remove the egg yolks and reserve the whites. Push the yolks through a sieve (strainer) into a bowl, then add the sugar, salt, mustard and lemon juice and blend together.

2 Whisk the cream in a bowl until it begins to thicken but is not stiff. Add to the egg mixture and mix to form a creamy dressing.

3 Arrange the salad leaves and cucumber slices on four individual serving plates and spoon over the salad cream. Chop the reserved egg whites and scatter over the top with the chopped herbs.

Per portion Energy 315kcal/1302kJ; Protein 4.8g; Carbohydrate 6.7g, of which sugars 6.6g; Fat 30.2g, of which saturates 17.5g; Cholesterol 164mg; Calcium 60mg; Fibre 0.5g; Sodium 405mg.

Serves 4

2 hard-boiled eggs

15ml/1 tbsp caster (superfine) sugar

2.5ml/½ tsp salt

15ml/1 tbsp Swedish or German mustard

30ml/2 tbsp lemon juice

200ml/7fl oz/scant 1 cup double (heavy) cream

summer salad leaves, such as little gem lettuce

½ cucumber, sliced

15ml/1 tbsp chopped fresh chives or dill

Variation Although not traditional, crème fraîche can be used to replace the cream, giving a slightly sharper finish to the dressing.

Serves 4

1 apple

3 cooked potatoes, finely diced

2 large gherkins, finely diced

3 cooked beetroots (beet), finely diced

3 cooked carrots, finely diced

1 onion, finely chopped

500ml/17fl oz/generous 2 cups double (heavy) cream

3 hard-boiled eggs, roughly chopped

15ml/1 tbsp chopped fresh parsley

salt and ground white pepper

Christmas beetroot, apple and potato salad
Rosolli

Rosolli is part of the traditional Christmas table – voileipäpöytä – Finland's equivalent of the Swedish smörgåsbord or Russian zakouski. It is served on Christmas Eve, just as the festive excitement mounts.

1 Cut the apple into small dice. Put in a bowl and add the potatoes, gherkins, beetroot, carrots and onion and season with salt and pepper. Carefully mix together and spoon into individual serving glasses or bowls.

2 Mix any beetroot juice into the cream to flavour and give it a pinkish colour, then spoon over the vegetables and apple. Sprinkle the chopped eggs and parsley on top before serving.

Per portion Energy 717kcal/2959kJ; Protein 8.5g; Carbohydrate 11g, of which sugars 10.2g; Fat 71.5g, of which saturates 42.9g; Cholesterol 314mg; Calcium 114mg; Fibre 2.3g; Sodium 132mg.

Variation Stir in ½ finely chopped salted herring fillet or 2 finely chopped anchovy fillets to the mixture with the parsley to add an extra dimension to the dish. Omit the added salt.

Serves 4

500g/1¼lb smoked eel fillet

5ml/1 tsp Swedish or German mustard

5ml/1 tsp grated fresh horseradish

about 50ml/2fl oz/¼ cup double
(heavy) cream

4 smoked sprats, skinned
and filleted

ground black pepper

lettuce and boiled new potatoes,
to serve

For the dressing

100ml/3½fl oz/scant ½ cup double
(heavy) cream

5ml/1 tsp mustard

5ml/1 tsp grated fresh horseradish

a little lemon juice

Variation The root of fresh horseradish
resembles a knobbly parsnip. It is very
versatile, and lends a pungent flavour
to vegetable, meat and fish dishes, as
well as making an excellent condiment.

Smoked fish salad
Savutettu kalasalaatti

*Oily fish – such as salmon, eels, sprats, perch, trout and herring – are well
suited to being smoked. The fish used in this recipe are hot-smoked, a
process that involves cooking and smoking the fish simultaneously over chips
of burning wood (such as alder, apple or juniper) or, more recently, in an
electric kiln. The smokiness and rich, oily flesh of the cooked fish is particularly
suited to sharp dressings and pungent, relish-type sauces, such as this simple
yet delicious horseradish and mustard one.*

1 Remove the skin from the smoked eel by peeling it off with your fingers, much
as you would skin a banana. Place the skinned, smoked eel on a board and cut
about half of it into four neat fillets. Set aside.

2 Put the remaining smoked eel fillet in a food processor, add the mustard and
horseradish and season with pepper. Blend until smooth, adding enough cream
to form a firm paste.

3 Spoon a dollop of the smoked eel paste or pâté on to a bed of lettuce on four
individual serving plates.

4 Carefully remove the skin from the smoked sprats using a small, sharp knife,
then arrange the skinned fish around the pâté, together with the reserved smoked
eel fillets.

5 To make the dressing, whisk together the cream, mustard, horseradish and a
few drops of lemon juice, until stiff. Spoon on to the salad and serve with boiled
new potatoes.

Per portion Energy 487kcal/2021kJ; Protein 30.8g; Carbohydrate 0.9g, of which sugars 0.7g; Fat 40.2g,
of which saturates 17.3g; Cholesterol 285mg; Calcium 94mg; Fibre 0g; Sodium 257mg.

Fish & shellfish

Salmon tartare

Salmon bake

Salmon and perch quenelle

Hot pot-smoked perch

Trout with cucumber
and horseradish

Fried sprats in rye flour

Baltic herring fillets with
caper butter sauce

Minced herring with blinis

Fish pie

Burbot chowder

White fish dumplings

Salmon, herring & rich sauces

Finland is reputed to have more than 60,000 lakes. Freshwater fish are, therefore, a staple of the Finnish kitchen. Although some of the prized species may be difficult to find outside Finland, salmon and trout, two of the most common, are widely available.

Finland's seaboard lies along the Baltic, as the strip of land connecting Finland to the Barents Sea and north Atlantic at Petsamo was forfeited to Russia after World War II. Salt levels in the Baltic are much lower than is usual in other seas and this affects the type and variety of fish found. Standard herrings and sprats can be used to replace the Baltic specimens in these recipes, although the taste will be slightly different.

The large, monkfish-like burbot (made) appears in the depths of Finnish lakes in the autumn and its liver and roe are considered a great delicacy. Vendace (muikku) are small sardine-shaped lake fish with a rich flavour. The species also has a larger variety, siika, which is sometimes available outside Finland.

Smoked, salted and pressed fish are standard mealtime items across northern Europe and every edible fish that is not eaten fresh is liable to undergo one or other of these treatments. These methods originated as means of preserving the fish before the days of refrigerators, but today they are used primarily because the salt and the smoke lend complexity and flavour to the fish.

Fresh dill is almost mandatory in most fish recipes in Finland, and it regularly appears as a pretty garnish even where it is not an integral ingredient in the dish itself.

Serves 4

400g/14oz Pressed Salmon with Dill
(see page 51)

grated rind of ½ lime or lemon

2.5ml/½ tsp ground black pepper

60ml/4 tbsp crème fraîche

15ml/1 tbsp chopped fresh dill,
plus a few sprigs to garnish

60ml/4 tbsp cream cheese, to serve

rye bread, to serve

Cook's tips

• Greek (US strained plain) yogurt can
be used in place of crème fraîche for
those who prefer the taste and,
conversely, sour cream can be used
for those who prefer a sharper, less
rich flavour.

• Raw fish, meat and eggs should not
be eaten by pregnant women, the
elderly, young children, or anyone with
an impaired immune system. Ensure
the fish used in this recipe is very fresh.

Salmon tartare
Lohitartari

*The base for this dish and for the Salmon Bake recipe is a lightly salted version
of gravlax, the Scandinavian dish of salmon marinated with dill. Steak Tartare is
a well-known dish, consisting of finely chopped, raw beef steak mixed with
capers, gherkins and anchovy, and served with raw egg yolk nestled in a dip in
the centre. The name "tartare" can, however, be applied to any uncooked and
chopped dish, including fish. Here, the pressing process acts in a similar way
to the cold-smoking of raw salmon, producing a delicate, subtly flavoured flesh.*

1 Thinly slice the Pressed Salmon with Dill into strips, reserving four small slices for
a garnish. Arrange these thin strips of salmon in a line on a large chopping board
and, using a large, sharp knife, cut them crossways into the finest small dice that
you can. Do not be tempted to use a food processor to do this, or you will end up
with salmon paste.

2 Put the chopped salmon in a large bowl and add the lime or lemon rind and the
pepper, then mix in half the crème fraîche.

3 Mould the salmon mixture into small burger-shaped patties, either by pushing the
mixture into round pastry cutters with a spoon to make neat rounds, or by shaping
it with wet hands for a more rustic finish.

4 Spread a thin coating of the remaining crème fraîche across the top of each
salmon mound. Top with one of the reserved salmon slices and add a sprig of dill
to garnish. Serve with cream cheese and rye bread.

Per portion Energy 253kcal/1050kJ; Protein 20.8g; Carbohydrate 0.1g, of which sugars 0.1g; Fat 18.8g;
of which saturates 6.8g; Cholesterol 66mg; Calcium 44mg; Fibre 0.2g; Sodium 92mg.

Salmon bake
Lohipaistos

Subtly flavoured with dill and onion, this warming bake combines two of the most common ingredients in Finland: salmon and potatoes. The recipe calls for graavilohi – salmon that has been pressed with salt, dill and brandy for 24 hours – which can be used in a number of recipes, or thinly sliced and simply served with a dill and crème fraîche sauce.

1 To make the Pressed Salmon and Dill, put the salt, sugar, dill, brandy and pepper in a bowl and mix together. Rub the mixture over both sides of the salmon fillets. Place the flesh sides of the fillets together, so that the skin sides are on the outside, to form a whole fish and wrap in foil.

2 Place the wrapped fish in a deep dish or roasting pan and place a heavy weight or weights, such as cans, on the top. Put in the refrigerator and leave for 12 hours. Turn the fish over, replace the weights and leave for a further 12 hours. Scrape off the marinade and pat the fish dry with kitchen paper.

3 To prepare the Salmon Bake, preheat the oven to 200°C/400°F/Gas 6. Grease a deep, ovenproof dish with a little of the butter.

4 Arrange half the potato slices in a layer over the base of the dish, then add a layer of salmon and a layer of onion. Sprinkle over the dill and end with a layer of the remaining potato slices.

5 Mix the eggs, milk, salt and pepper together and pour over the dish. Dot the remaining butter on top. Bake in the oven for 1 hour, until the potatoes are tender. Serve immediately.

Serves 4

25g/1oz/2 tbsp unsalted (sweet) butter, softened

8 potatoes, thinly sliced

300g/11oz Pressed Salmon with Dill, sliced (see below)

1 onion, finely chopped

30ml/2 tbsp chopped fresh dill

3 eggs, beaten

400ml/14fl oz/1⅔ cups milk

5ml/1 tsp salt

2.5ml/½ tsp ground white pepper

For the Pressed Salmon with Dill (Graavilohi)

90ml/6 tbsp coarse sea salt

90ml/6 tbsp sugar

90ml/6 tbsp chopped fresh dill

30ml/2 tbsp brandy

5ml/1 tsp ground black pepper

1 small or ½ large fresh salmon, filleted

Cook's tip To make a simple dill and crème fraîche sauce, heat 25ml/ 1½ tbsp fish stock or white wine and 1 peeled, chopped shallot in a large pan until they come to the boil. Add 100g/3¾oz/scant ½ cup crème fraîche and bring back to the boil. Stir in 15ml/1 tbsp dill leaves, then check the seasoning, adding salt and pepper as required.

Per portion Energy 338kcal/1413kJ; Protein 24.3g; Carbohydrate 17.9g, of which sugars 10.2g; Fat 19.4g, of which saturates 7g; Cholesterol 199mg; Calcium 167mg; Fibre 0.7g; Sodium 665mg.

Salmon and perch quenelle
Lohi- ja ahvenkerros

This delectable spinach, fish and mushroom dish is cooked in the shape of a tart and is best served hot, cut into generous wedges. A flavoursome crayfish sauce makes a good accompaniment.

1 Cook the spinach, in only the water clinging to its leaves after washing, for 5 minutes, until wilted. Drain, then rinse the spinach under cold running water. Drain well and squeeze out as much water as possible.

2 Melt 50g/2oz/¼ cup of the butter in a pan, add the onion and fry for 5 minutes until softened. Add the mushrooms and cook until any liquid that the mushrooms produce has evaporated. Add the spinach then season well with salt, pepper and nutmeg. Leave to cool.

3 Cut the perch fillets into small dice and season with salt, pepper and nutmeg. Chill in the freezer for 10 minutes.

4 Put the fish in the bowl of a food processor and blend to form a purée, adding the egg whites, one at a time. In a slow trickle, finally add the cream and season.

5 Preheat the oven to 180°C/350°F/Gas 4. Use the remaining butter to grease a 24cm/9½in round cake tin (pan). Spread the spinach over the base of the tin, then spread half the fish mixture on top. Place the salmon slices on top, then spread the remaining fish mixture over the slices. Tap the sides of the tin to ensure that there are no gaps between layers. Cover with lightly buttered baking parchment.

6 Place the tin in a deep roasting pan and half fill with warm water. Bake for about 50 minutes or until a skewer inserted in the centre comes out clean.

7 Meanwhile, make the Crayfish Sauce. Bring a large pan of salted water to the boil. Twist the centre segment of each crayfish tail and pull out the waste canal. Drop the crayfish into the water and cook for 4 minutes. Drain and refresh the shellfish in cold water, then peel, reserving the shells and bodies.

8 Heat the butter in a large frying pan, add the chopped onion and fry for 3 minutes, without colouring. Add the debris and shells from the crayfish and continue to fry for a further 2–3 minutes, then add the brandy.

9 Stir in the passata and the flour and continue to cook for another minute. Add the stock, bring to the boil, then simmer for 10 minutes. Add the cream, lemon and seasonings, then strain the liquid into a clean pan. Return the crayfish meat to the warm sauce and garnish with dill.

10 Turn the quenelle out of the tin so that the spinach is on top, and serve immediately with the Crayfish Sauce.

Serves 6

600g/1lb 6oz spinach, washed

100g/3¾oz/scant ½ cup butter

1 onion, chopped

200g/7oz button (white) mushrooms, thinly sliced

grated nutmeg

500g/1¼lb perch fillets

3 egg whites

400ml14fl oz/1⅔ cups double (heavy) cream

500g/1¼lb salmon fillet, sliced

salt and ground black pepper

For the Crayfish Sauce

12 crayfish

25g/1oz/2 tbsp unsalted (sweet) butter

1 small onion, peeled and chopped

15ml/1 tbsp brandy

15ml/1 tbsp passata (bottled strained tomatoes)

5ml/1 tsp plain (all-purpose) flour

105ml/7 tbsp fish or chicken stock

25ml/1½ tbsp double (heavy) cream

few drops lemon juice

salt and tabasco or cayenne pepper

dill, to garnish

Per portion Energy 406kcal/1687kJ; Protein 38.1g; Carbohydrate 2.6g, of which sugars 2.2g; Fat 27g, of which saturates 10.4g; Cholesterol 77mg; Calcium 203mg; Fibre 2.6g; Sodium 358mg.

Hot pot-smoked perch
Padassa savustettu ahven

Hot-smoking cooks the fish as well as flavouring it. The smoking process is in fact a controlled form of tainting and the type of wood used will affect the flavour.

1 Place a lining of foil in the base of a wok or pan, then pile on the rice and sugar. Mix the tea leaves with the juniper berries, then pour on top of the rice and sugar. Place a trivet in the wok or pan so that it stands above the mixture.

2 Season the fish with salt and pepper and add the lemon juice, then place on the trivet. Cover with a tight fitting lid and turn on the heat at maximum. The smoke that rises will flavour and cook the fish and the pressure that builds up will speed up the process. Allow 25–30 minutes for a 1kg/2¼lb fish and 15–20 minutes for anything smaller.

3 Serve hot, with a green salad and boiled new potatoes.

Per portion Energy 223kcal/939kJ; Protein 38.8g; Carbohydrate 0.1g, of which sugars 0.1g; Fat 7.5g, of which saturates 1.8g; Cholesterol 160mg; Calcium 60mg; Fibre 0g; Sodium 145mg.

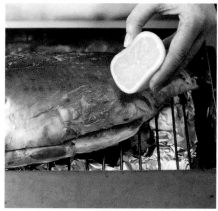

Serves 4

100g/3¾oz/½ cup rice

100g/3¾oz/½ cup sugar

50g/1oz tea leaves

50g/1oz juniper berries

1kg/2¼lb perch, cleaned and scaled, or any whole small to medium fish or large fillets or chunks, such as salmon

a few drops of lemon juice

salt and ground black pepper

salads and boiled new potatoes, to serve

Cook's tip This recipe would traditionally use juniper twigs instead of the rice, sugar, tea and juniper berries.

Serves 4

1 cucumber, thinly sliced

75g/3oz/6 tbsp butter, softened, plus extra for greasing

5ml/1 tsp Dijon mustard

20g/¾oz grated horseradish

a few drops of lemon juice

600g/1lb 6oz trout fillet, cut into twelve 50g/2oz thin slices

45ml/3 tbsp water or white wine

salt and ground black pepper

Trout with cucumber and horseradish
Taimen kurkun ja piparjuuren kanssa

Horseradish is one of the principal aromatics in Finnish cooking. Used with care, it gives zest to a dish rather than overpowers it. If you are able to use fresh horseradish and grate it yourself, so much the better.

1 Sprinkle the cucumber slices with 2.5ml/½ tsp salt and mix together. Sandwich the slices between two plates, place a small weight on top and leave in the refrigerator for 30 minutes. Squeeze out any juices from the cucumber.

2 Preheat the oven to 200°C/400°F/Gas 6. Grease a shallow, ovenproof dish with butter and sprinkle a little salt over the base. Put the softened butter in a bowl and beat until it is light and fluffy, then add the mustard, horseradish, lemon juice and a little pepper, and beat until well mixed.

3 Arrange the trout slices in the prepared dish in four servings, each consisting of three overlapping slices. Spread these with the horseradish butter. Arrange the cucumber slices across the top of each serving, to look like fish scales.

4 Add water or white wine to the dish, then cover with foil. Bake in the oven for 6–7 minutes until just tender. Using a fish slice, carefully transfer each serving to a warmed plate and serve hot.

Per portion Energy 314kcal/1306kJ; Protein 29.7g; Carbohydrate 1g, of which sugars 0.9g; Fat 21.3g, of which saturates 9.8g; Cholesterol 40mg; Calcium 27mg; Fibre 0.3g; Sodium 236mg.

Cook's tip It is very easy to overcook trout, which makes it dry. You need to remember that residual heat on the outside of the fish will continue to cook the centre for as long as it remains warm, so it should be served as soon as it is ready.

Fried sprats in rye flour
Silakkapihvit

Baltic sprats have soft bones, like sardines, so they can be eaten without discomfort if you don't want to pick them out.

1 To make the Tartare Sauce, whisk the egg yolks, mustard and vinegar in a bowl. Slowly add the oil, drop by drop at first, then, when it begins to thicken, in a slow, steady stream, whisking all the time until it begins to thicken like mayonnaise. Stir in the anchovy essence, chopped gherkin, capers and parsley into the sauce and season to taste with salt and pepper. Store in the refrigerator until ready to use.

2 To prepare the sprats, cut off the head and tail, make a slit along the belly and remove the guts. Cut the backbone near the head and remove the backbone. Open the fish out like a book. Season the insides of the fish with salt and pepper and sprinkle over the chopped chives. Place two fish together so that the flesh sides are pressed against one another and the skin sides are on the outside.

3 Break the egg on to a plate and beat together with the milk. Spread the rye flour and the breadcrumbs on separate plates. Dip the pairs of fish in the rye flour, to coat on both sides, then in the beaten egg and finally the breadcrumbs.

4 Heat the oil in a large frying pan, add the coated fish and fry for about 5 minutes on each side until crisp and tender. Serve hot, with the Tartare Sauce.

Per portion Energy 592kcal/2466kJ; Protein 18.8g; Carbohydrate 39.2g, of which sugars 1.7g; Fat 41g, of which saturates 5.7g; Cholesterol 156mg; Calcium 141mg; Fibre 1.3g; Sodium 601mg.

Serves 4

8 sprats

60ml/4 tbsp chopped fresh chives

1 egg

45ml/3 tbsp milk

50g/2oz/½ cup rye flour

200g/7oz/4 cups fine fresh breadcrumbs

vegetable oil, for shallow frying

salt and ground white pepper

For the Tartare Sauce

2 egg yolks

15ml/1 tbsp Swedish or German mustard

15ml/1 tbsp white wine vinegar

200ml/7fl oz/scant 1 cup vegetable oil

5ml/1 tsp anchovy essence (paste)

15ml/1 tbsp chopped gherkin

15ml/1 tbsp chopped capers

15ml/1 tbsp chopped fresh parsley

salt and ground black pepper

Baltic herring fillets with caper butter sauce
Silli kapriskastikkeen kanssa

This recipe is a modern take on a traditional recipe using Baltic herrings. In earlier years, no Finn would waste vodka in cooking, mostly because it was too expensive and hard to come by. The flavour of the ubiquitous dill adds that authentic Finnish flavour to this otherwise simple dish.

1 Preheat the oven to 200°C/400°F/Gas 6. Grease a shallow, ovenproof dish with butter and sprinkle 15ml/1 tbsp of the breadcrumbs over the base.

2 To make the Caper Butter, put the softened butter in a bowl and beat until it is light and fluffy, then whisk in the vodka, dill, capers and cayenne pepper.

3 Season the fish with salt then fold each fillet in half, so that the skin sides are on the outside. Lightly press the folded fish together with your fingers. Arrange the fillets in the prepared dish.

4 Spread the Caper Butter over the fish, then sprinkle over the remaining breadcrumbs. Bake the fish in the oven for 25 minutes or until the top is crisp and golden brown.

Per portion Energy 545kcal/2261kJ; Protein 28.6g; Carbohydrate 10.1g, of which sugars 0.7g; Fat 42.8g, of which saturates 19.3g; Cholesterol 134mg; Calcium 126mg; Fibre 0.7g; Sodium 444mg.

Serves 4

a little butter, for greasing

50g/2oz/1 cup fine fresh breadcrumbs

600g/1lb 6oz Baltic herring fillets

salt

For the Caper Butter Sauce

100g/3¾oz/scant ½ cup butter, softened

15ml/1 tbsp vodka

30ml/2 tbsp chopped fresh dill

15ml/1 tbsp capers

1 large pinch cayenne pepper

Cook's tip For a truly authentic flavour, use Finnish vodka.

Serves 4

1 salted herring, cut into two fillets

about 10ml/2 tsp double (heavy) cream

2 hard-boiled eggs, chopped

½ onion, very finely chopped

15ml/1 tbsp fine fresh breadcrumbs

2.5ml/½ tsp mustard (see Cook's tip)

15ml/1 tbsp chopped fresh parsley

about 5ml/1 tsp caster (superfine) sugar

ground white pepper

For the Blinis

450ml/15fl oz/scant 2 cups milk

25g/1oz fresh yeast

60g/2¼oz/generorus ½ cup buckwheat flour

about 90g/3½oz/¾ cup plain (all-purpose) flour

40g/1½oz/3 tbsp butter

5ml/1 tsp salt

2 eggs, separated, plus 2 egg whites

butter or vegetable oil, for shallow frying

Cook's tip Scandinavia uses mild mustard rather than the powerful English variety. Try to source Swedish mustard or, failing that, use a German or Dijon mustard.

Minced herring with blinis
Sillikaviaari

Herring, like caviar, has a pronounced fish taste and the ingredients mixed into this paste are the same as those traditionally served with caviar. Warm, freshly cooked blinis make an ideal accompaniment. Serve as an appetizer on their own or as part of a light lunch with a crunchy green salad.

1 Soak the herring fillets in cold water for at least 2–3 hours or, preferably, overnight. Remove the skin then chop the flesh very finely or mince (grind).

2 Add enough cream to the minced (ground) fish to form a paste, then add the hard-boiled eggs, onion, breadcrumbs, mustard and parsley. Add the sugar to taste and season with pepper.

3 To make the blinis, put 250ml/8fl oz/1 cup of the milk in a pan and heat gently until just warm to the touch. Put the yeast in a small bowl, and pour over the warm milk. Blend the yeast with the milk, then add the buckwheat flour and 30g/1¼oz/ generous ¼ cup of the plain flour and mix together. Cover the bowl and leave the mixture to prove at room temperature for 1 hour.

4 Melt the butter in a pan, then leave to cool. Pour the remaining 200ml/7fl oz/ scant 1 cup milk into a small pan and heat until just warm to the touch. Whisk the warm milk into the yeast mixture. Stir in enough of the remaining plain flour to form a thick paste.

5 Add the salt to the mixture, then beat in the egg yolks and melted butter. Whisk all the egg whites until stiff, then fold into the batter.

6 Heat the butter or oil in a frying pan, add a tablespoonful of batter at a time and fry for 4 minutes, turning once, to make about 16 small, slightly risen blinis. Serve hot, with the minced herring.

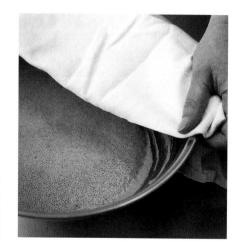

Per portion Energy 443kcal/1851kJ; Protein 16.4g; Carbohydrate 40.7g, of which sugars 7.7g; Fat 25.2g, of which saturates 9.1g; Cholesterol 221mg; Calcium 212mg; Fibre 1.3g; Sodium 737mg.

Fish pie
Kalakukko

The rather everyday title of Fish Pie doesn't do justice to this famous dish from Savo. It is made with small freshwater fish called vendace, known as muikku in Finnish, and belly pork, wrapped in a rye crust. Small perch or sprats can be substituted for the vendace if you are unable to find the authentic ingredient.

1 To make the dough, put the milk in a pan and heat gently until just warm to the touch. Put the yeast in a small bowl, and pour over the warm milk. Blend the yeast with the milk, then leave in a warm place for about 15 minutes until the yeast begins to bubble. Meanwhile, melt the butter in a small pan and leave to cool.

2 Put 400g/14oz/3½ cups of the rye flour in a large bowl, add the salt, milk and yeast mixture, water and melted butter and mix together to form a soft dough. Cover the bowl and leave at room temperature for 30 minutes until doubled in size.

3 Preheat the oven to 240°C/475°F/Gas 9. Add the remaining rye flour and the plain flour to the risen mixture to make a stiff dough. Turn on to a lightly floured surface and knead for about 10 minutes, until smooth and elastic. Turn the dough on to baking parchment and roll out the rye dough to a 20cm x 20cm/8in x 8in rectangle, 1cm/½in in thickness. Place on a baking sheet.

4 Arrange the fish in layers in the centre of the dough, all facing the same direction and alternating with the slices of belly pork. Season each layer with salt. Lift the edges of the dough up and over the filling, overlapping them if possible. Brush the edges of the pastry with water to moisten, then pinch together firmly to seal.

5 Bake the pie in the oven for 30 minutes, then lower the oven temperature to 150°C/300°F/Gas 2. Remove the pie from the oven, brush with the cooled, melted butter and cover with moistened baking parchment and then with foil. Return the pie to the oven and bake for at least a further 3 hours.

6 Remove the pie from the oven and cover with a wet dish towel to soften the crust. Leave for 15 minutes if serving hot. If serving cold, chill in the refrigerator overnight so that the filling sets.

Serves 4

1kg/2¼lb vendace or perch, cleaned, gutted and heads removed

150g/5oz sliced belly pork

15ml/1 tbsp salt

a little melted butter, to glaze

For the dough

25ml/1½ tbsp milk

25g/1oz fresh yeast

50g/2oz/¼ cup butter

450g/1lb/4 cups rye flour

5ml/1 tsp salt

500ml/17fl oz/generous 2 cups cold water

50g/2oz/½ cup plain (all-purpose) flour

Per portion Energy 862kcal/3634kJ; Protein 55.2g; Carbohydrate 95.5g, of which sugars 0.6g; Fat 31.6g, of which saturates 12.3g; Cholesterol 209mg; Calcium 126mg; Fibre 13.6g; Sodium 1711mg.

Cook's tip Rye dough is very sticky to handle, but you can use plenty of plain (all-purpose) flour at every stage of the process to make handling easier. Sprinkle the flour on each surface and over the rolling pin.

Serves 4

1kg/2¼lb burbot or monkfish, with their bones, if filleted

20g/¾oz/1½ tbsp unsalted (sweet) butter

1 onion, chopped

1 small celery stick, chopped

1 small leek, chopped

1 bay leaf

10 whole allspice

5 white peppercorns

1.5 litres/2½ pints/6¼ cups water

1 carrot, finely diced

500g/1¼lb potatoes, cubed

5ml/1 tsp plain white (all-purpose) flour

200ml/7fl oz/scant 1 cup double (heavy) cream

salt and ground white pepper

dill sprigs, to garnish

Cook's tips

• Cooked fish trimmings retain a lot of well-flavoured liquid, so when you have strained the stock, allow the trimmings to rest and release further stock.

• If you use monkfish, ask your fishmonger for some extra fish bones or heads.

Burbot chowder
Madekeitto

Burbot is a large freshwater fish that looks similar to a monkfish, and which has soft but well-flavoured flesh. In fact, years ago, their similarity led to both fish being called burbot. This hearty chowder can be served on its own as a tasty appetizer or with bread for a sustaining main meal.

1 Fillet the fish or, if the fishmonger fillets it for you, ask him to reserve the bones and head. Cut the fish into large chunks.

2 Heat the butter in a pan, add the chopped onion, celery, leek, fish bones, fish head and any fish trimmings. Fry for about 5 minutes until the vegetables are beginning to soften. Add the bay leaf, allspice, peppercorns, 15ml/1 tbsp salt and 1 litre/1¾ pints/4 cups of the water. Bring to the boil, then lower the heat and simmer very gently for 30 minutes.

3 Strain the stock through a sieve (strainer) into a clean pan. (You should be left with about 1 litre/1¾ pints/4 cups of liquid. If you do not have enough, add extra water to make up the correct amount.)

4 Add the carrot and potato to the stock and bring to the boil. Lower the heat and simmer until the potato is nearly cooked. The timing will vary depending upon the size of the potato cubes and the variety of the potato.

5 Add the fish to the pan and return to simmering point, then sprinkle over the flour and continue to simmer for a further 5 minutes, or until the fish is just cooked.

6 Stir in the cream, then taste and add salt and pepper according to taste. Pour into individual serving dishes and serve hot, garnished with a sprig of dill.

Per portion Energy 582kcal/2431kJ; Protein 47.6g; Carbohydrate 25.8g, of which sugars 6.4g; Fat 32.6g, of which saturates 19.7g; Cholesterol 119mg; Calcium 77mg; Fibre 2.8g; Sodium 117mg.

White fish dumplings
Kalapyörykät

Served on a bed of summer vegetables with a creamy white wine sauce, these fish dumplings are best made with dry-fleshed white fish such as pike or possibly perch, although hake or brill also both produce good results.

1 Cut the fish into small dice, put in the bowl of a food processor and blend until finely chopped, slowly adding the egg whites, salt, pepper and cayenne pepper while blending. Put the fish paste in a bowl and place in the freezer for 20 minutes, until very cold but not frozen. Beat in 100ml/3½fl oz/scant ½ cup of the cream, then set aside in the refrigerator.

2 Heat the oil in a pan, add the onion and celery and fry for about 5 minutes, until softened but not browned. Add the fish bones and continue to cook for 10 minutes, until they start to smell cooked rather than raw. Pour in half of the white wine and enough water to just cover the bones. Bring to the boil, then reduce the heat and simmer for 20 minutes. Strain the stock through a sieve (strainer) into a clean pan. You should have about 400ml/14fl oz/1⅔ cups fish stock.

3 Bring the stock to a gentle simmer. Use two tablespoons to shape the fish mixture into balls and drop these into the boiling stock in two or three batches. Cook for about 5 minutes, turning them over gently during cooking. Using a slotted spoon, transfer to an ovenproof dish and keep warm in a cool oven.

4 Melt the butter in a pan, stir in the flour to make a roux that comes cleanly away from the pan base as it is stirred, then stir in a ladleful of the fish stock. Slowly bring to the boil, stirring all the time, until the sauce boils and thickens. Repeat the process until the sauce has a smooth, velvet texture.

5 Stir the remaining wine and the remaining cream into the sauce, return to the boil then remove from the heat. Whisk in the egg yolks and dill, then taste and add salt and pepper according to taste. Pour the sauce over the dumplings and serve hot, on a bed of cooked early summer vegetables.

Serves 4

500g/1¼lb white fish fillets, plus their bones

2 eggs, separated

5ml/1 tsp salt

2.5ml/½ tsp ground white pepper

a pinch of cayenne pepper

200ml/7fl oz/scant 1 cup double (heavy) cream

25ml/1½ tbsp vegetable oil

1 onion, chopped

1 small celery stick, chopped

300ml/½ pint/1¼ cups white wine

50g/2oz/¼ cup unsalted (sweet) butter

30ml/2 tbsp plain (all-purpose) flour

15ml/1 tbsp chopped fresh dill

salt and ground black or white pepper

cooked early summer vegetables, such as young carrots, peas, asparagus and spinach, to serve

Cook's tip Be sure to ask your fishmonger to remove the pinbones that run along the length of the fish or, alternatively, use tweezers to pull them out yourself.

Per portion Energy 600kcal/2484kJ; Protein 27.7g; Carbohydrate 6.5g, of which sugars 2.4g; Fat 46.4g, of which saturates 24.8g; Cholesterol 248mg; Calcium 73mg; Fibre 0.5g; Sodium 205mg.

Meat & game

Reindeer, elk & domestic meat

Finns have traditionally eaten their meat either completely cooked through, or raw as steak tartare. The dishes from Finland that date back centuries are usually stews and casseroles, enriched and enlivened by aromatics, spices and herbs – including horseradish, allspice or dill. The influences from the east, especially in Karelian dishes, originated from neighbouring Russia. In Finland, as in Russia, meat was scarce and expensive. The working man's ration would therefore be extended by the judicious use of rye crusts and potato, or maybe rice. This tradition has survived, and many casseroles and hot-pots still contain root vegetables, such as celeriac, potato and carrot, as well earthy, flavoursome wild mushrooms when they are in season.

The furred game that is available in Finland, including elk and reindeer, is largely specific to the far northern hemisphere and especially Lapland. Here, hares have adapted to the climate, turning white in the winter to blend with the snow. These, like wild ducks, are hunted in autumn and winter. Reindeer is sold as butcher's meat, ideal for stewing, or smoked and sliced as charcuterie. The tongues are considered a delicacy and are made into pâtés and terrines.

There is a great range of pork products available, and every part of the pig is eaten, including the liver, trotters and blood. Sausages are a national favourite, and taste particularly wonderful with a glass of Lapin kulta or Lahden beer, and it is a strong reminder of the backwoodsman-quality that flows through much of Finland's character and food.

Elk and celeriac casserole
Hirvipata

Elks are large animals, cousins of the North American moose, just as reindeer are related to caribou. The meat is dark and tastes similar to venison, which can be used as a good substitute if you are unable to buy elk meat. Serve this rich, warming stew on its own or, for a more sustaining meal, with creamy mashed potatoes or lightly boiled new potatoes, and some steamed green vegetables, such as cabbage, broccoli or spinach.

1 Preheat the oven to 180°C/350°F/Gas 4. Cut the elk meat into chunky cubes, then season salt and pepper.

2 Heat the lard or oil in a flameproof and ovenproof dish, then add the meat, chopped onions and chopped carrots. Fry the meat and vegetables until the vegetables soften and the meat is brown on all sides.

3 Add the water, celeriac and juniper berries to the pan, bring to the boil then cover. Cook in the oven for about 2 hours, until the meat is tender.

4 Remove the casserole from the oven and dust the surface of the liquid with the flour, and stir to combine with and thicken the sauce. Return the dish to the oven and cook for a further 10 minutes.

5 Stir in the blackcurrant jelly and the wine vinegar. If necessary, adjust the consistency by adding a little more water. Taste and add salt and pepper if needed.

6 Finally, stir in the butter until it has melted and is completely incorporated. Serve the casserole immediately.

Serves 4

1kg/2¼lb boneless elk, preferably from the hindquarter

25g/1oz/2 tbsp lard or 30ml/2 tbsp vegetable oil

2 onions, roughly chopped

2 carrots, roughly chopped

750ml/1¼ pints/3 cups water

1 small celeriac, cubed

8 juniper berries

30ml/2 tbsp plain (all-purpose) flour

15ml/1 tbsp blackcurrant jelly

15ml/1 tbsp wine vinegar

25g/1oz/2 tbsp unsalted (sweet) butter

salt and ground black pepper

Cook's tip The addition of the butter improves the texture of the cooking liquid and adds a touch of creaminess to the dense meat.

Per portion Energy 452kcal/1901kJ; Protein 58g; Carbohydrate 20.8g, of which sugars 12.5g; Fat 17.4g, of which saturates 7.9g; Cholesterol 144mg; Calcium 83mg; Fibre 3.4g; Sodium 222mg.

Roast elk with cabbage cream tart
Paistettu hirvi

Elk can become dry if it is roasted for too long, so make sure that you serve it rare or medium rare. Here, the tender meat is served with a creamy tart.

1 Preheat the oven to 200°C/400°F/Gas 6. Season the meat with salt and pepper then brush with the goose fat or oil. Toss the meat in a large frying pan and sear so that it is browned on both sides, then transfer to a roasting pan.

2 Roast the elk or beef in the oven for about 25 minutes, according to how well-done you like your meat, then remove from the oven and keep warm. Reduce the oven temperature to 180°C/350°F/Gas 4.

3 Meanwhile, make the tart. Heat the goose fat in a pan, add the onion and cabbage and fry for about 5 minutes, until softened but not browned. Add the rosemary and season with salt and pepper.

4 Sift the flour, baking powder and salt into a bowl. Add the butter and mashed potato and mix together until combined. Knead with your hands two or three times in the bowl to form a smooth dough.

5 On a lightly floured surface, roll out the dough then use it to line a 20cm/8in non-stick flan tin (pan). Cover the pastry with baking parchment and fill with dried beans or rice, then cook in the oven for 20 minutes.

6 Meanwhile, whisk the eggs in a bowl with the sour cream, salt and pepper. Remove the baking parchment and beans or rice from the pastry, and add the cabbage mixture to the tart case.

7 Pour in the egg mixture, then bake the tart in the oven for 30 minutes, until set. Serve hot, cut into wedges, with the roast meat.

Serves 4

800g/1¾lb fillet of elk or beef, from the saddle

25g/1oz/2 tbsp goose fat or 30ml/2 tbsp vegetable oil

For the tart

25g/1oz/2 tbsp goose fat

1 onion, sliced

400g/14oz white cabbage, thinly sliced

5ml/1 tsp fresh rosemary leaves, chopped

100g/3¾oz/scant ½ cup plain (all-purpose) flour

5ml/1 tsp baking powder

5ml/1 tsp salt

100g/3¾oz/scant ½ cup butter, softened

150g/5oz mashed potato (see Cook's Tip)

2 eggs

200ml/7fl oz/scant 1 cup sour cream

salt and ground black pepper

Per portion Energy 780kcal/3256kJ; Protein 53.7g; Carbohydrate 33.7g, of which sugars 8.7g; Fat 50g, of which saturates 24.9g; Cholesterol 284mg; Calcium 166mg; Fibre 3.5g; Sodium 821mg.

Cook's tips
• To make 150g/5oz mashed potato, boil 200g/7oz potatoes in a pan of lightly salted water, then mash with 25g/1oz/2 tbsp butter and 75ml/5 tbsp milk until the mixture is smooth.
• The pan juices will make a good sauce. Add a glass of red wine and a little water to the roasting pan once the meat has cooked and bring to the boil. Thicken with 5ml/1 tsp potato flour or cornflour (cornstarch) mixed with 15ml/1 tbsp water, then strain into a jug (pitcher) or over the meat.

Serves 6

400g/14oz pork shoulder, diced

400g/14oz chuck beef, diced

400g/14oz lamb shoulder, diced

5ml/1 tsp ground allspice

2 onions, chopped

2 carrots, diced

½ small swede (rutabaga), diced

750ml/1¼ pints/3 cups water

salt and ground black pepper

rye bread and mashed potatoes,
to serve

Karelian hot-pot
Karjalanpaisti

This eastern Finnish hot-pot uses three different types of meat, which are slow-cooked together. In the past, this dish would have been taken to the village baker and cooked in his oven once the day's bread had been baked.

1 Preheat the oven to 150°C/300°F/Gas 2. Season the meat with salt, pepper and allspice, then layer the meat with the onions, carrots and swede in a casserole.

2 Bring the water to the boil, then pour into the dish. Cover and cook in the oven for about 5 hours or until the meat is very tender. The cooking time will vary, depending upon the size of the meat cubes. Test for tenderness after 3 hours and then about every 30 minutes.

3 Serve hot, with rye bread and mashed potatoes.

Per portion Energy 335kcal/1400kJ; Protein 42.9g; Carbohydrate 3.8g, of which sugars 3.4g; Fat 16.5g, of which saturates 7g; Cholesterol 131mg; Calcium 38mg; Fibre 1.2g; Sodium 156mg.

Serves 4

25g/1oz dried morel mushrooms

100ml/3½fl oz/scant ½ cup plus 15ml/1 tbsp water

1 shallot, finely chopped

5ml/1 tsp potato flour

45ml/3 tbsp crème fraîche

1 gherkin, thinly sliced lengthways

4 boneless steaks cut from saddles of reindeer (caribou) or another type of venison, about 200g/7oz each

vegetable oil, for grilling or frying

25g/1oz/2 tbsp unsalted (sweet) butter

salt and ground black pepper

Cook's tip Morel mushrooms, even dried ones, can be gritty, so leave the cooking liquid a few minutes after straining them so that any grit sinks to the bottom. Strain most of the liquid into a clean pan, leaving the grit behind in the liquid that remains.

Reindeer fillet with morel mushrooms
Poro sienikastikkeessa

Reindeer, like elk, should not be overcooked or the meat can become tough. Here, the fillet is pan-fried and served with a creamy morel mushroom sauce. Morel mushrooms grow in early summer, ahead of the main fungus season. Often sold in their dried form, they are one of the finest mushroom varieties and lend a distinct and individual flavour to any dish.

1 Put the morels in a pan, add the 100ml/3½fl oz/scant ½ cup water and bring to the boil. Remove from the heat and leave to cool. Once cool, strain the liquid into a clean pan, reserving the morels. Add the shallot to the pan.

2 Put the potato flour in a bowl, add the 15ml/1 tbsp water and blend together. Add the mixture to the pan and bring to the boil, stirring all the time, until slightly thickened. Carefully strain the sauce into a clean pan, then add the reserved morels, crème fraîche and gherkin.

3 Brush the reindeer or other venison steaks with oil, then season with salt and pepper. Grill (broil) or fry the steaks for about 5 minutes, depending on how rare you like your meat.

4 Whisk any cooking juices from the steaks into the sauce along with the unsalted butter and reheat gently. Serve the steaks, accompanied by the morel sauce.

Per portion Energy 357kcal/1495kJ; Protein 45.2g; Carbohydrate 2.8g, of which sugars 1.3g; Fat 19.6g, of which saturates 8.6g; Cholesterol 126mg; Calcium 25mg; Fibre 0.4g; Sodium 152mg.

Serves 4

500g/1¼lb reindeer (caribou) or venison bones

1 calf's foot, split

4 litres/7 pints/16 cups water

1 onion, roughly chopped

5ml/1 tsp ground allspice

500g/1¼lb boneless venison meat, preferably shoulder

2 carrots, cut into large dice

1 celery stick, cut into 5cm/2in lengths

4 potatoes, cut into large dice

25g/1oz pearl barley

1 leek, cut into 5cm/2in lengths

15ml/1 tbsp chopped fresh parsley

salt and ground black pepper

Cook's tip Slow-cooking is the key to this dish. The meat will remain moist and tender provided it is not boiled too rapidly.

Reindeer pot-au-feu
Poronkeitto

The name of this dish gives some indication of the influence of foreign cultures on Finnish cuisine, although the ingredients remain authentically Scandinavian. Reindeer bones give plenty of flavour but little of the desirable gelatinous quality of veal bones. This recipe calls for a calf's foot to be used to give the best of both worlds, but can be omitted, if preferred. If you are unable to buy venison bones, veal bones or even chicken bones can be substituted.

1 Preheat the oven to 200°C/400°F/Gas 6. Put the reindeer or venison bones and calf's foot in a roasting pan and roast in the oven for about 30 minutes until lightly browned. Take care not to burn the bones or the stock will taste bitter.

2 Transfer the venison bones, calf's foot and pan juices to a large pan. Add the water, onion and allspice, bring to the boil, then reduce the heat and simmer for at least 2 hours. Skim away any froth that rises to the surface.

3 Strain the stock into a clean pan. Add the reindeer or other venison and simmer gently for 1½ hours. Skim away any froth that rises to the surface.

4 Add the carrots and celery to the pan and simmer for 10 minutes. Add the potatoes and barley and simmer for a further 10 minutes.

5 Finally, add the leek and simmer until the potato and barley are tender. Add the chopped parsley and season with salt and pepper.

6 To serve, remove the cooked meat from the pan and slice into thick portions. Place slices of meat in individual, warmed, deep serving dishes or bowls and add a ladleful of the cooking liquid.

Per portion Energy 496kcal/2110kJ; Protein 36.6g; Carbohydrate 83.9g, of which sugars 7.5g; Fat 4.7g, of which saturates 1.3g; Cholesterol 63mg; Calcium 58mg; Fibre 4g; Sodium 106mg.

Serves 4

150g/5oz mushrooms, finely chopped

50g/2oz/1 cup fine fresh breadcrumbs

100ml/3½fl oz/scant ½ cup double (heavy) cream

250g/9oz minced (ground) beef

1 onion, chopped

1 egg, beaten

5ml/1 tsp chopped rosemary leaves

5ml/1 tsp salt

1.5ml/¼ tsp ground white pepper

15g/½oz/1 tbsp butter, for greasing

creamed mushrooms (see Cook's tip) and tossed salads, to serve

Beef and mushroom meatloaf
Sieni- ja lihamureke

Ideally, this mushroom and minced beef dish will include woodland mushrooms, such as cep or girolle, but cultivated mushrooms are also very good. Use flat rather than button mushrooms, as they have more flavour. The same mixture can also be formed into patties and fried in a little butter.

1 Preheat the oven to 200°C/400°F/Gas 6. Grease a 450g/1lb loaf tin (pan) or small, deep ovenproof dish.

2 Put the mushrooms in a bowl. Add the breadcrumbs and cream and mix together. Add the minced beef, onion, egg, rosemary, salt and pepper and knead the ingredients together into a ball.

3 Transfer the mixture to the prepared tin or dish, cover with foil and bake in the oven for 40 minutes, until it feels firm when pressed with an upturned fork or spoon.

4 Turn out the meatloaf and serve hot, with creamed mushrooms or tossed salad.

Per portion Energy 366kcal/1517kJ; Protein 16.6g; Carbohydrate 11.5g, of which sugars 1.7g; Fat 28.5g, of which saturates 15.1g; Cholesterol 127mg; Calcium 48mg; Fibre 0.9g; Sodium 684mg.

Cook's tip To make creamed mushrooms, boil 200g/7oz sliced button (white) mushrooms with 100ml/3½fl oz/scant ½ cup double (heavy) cream for about 5 minutes, or until the mushrooms are tender. Season to taste with salt, ground black pepper and grated nutmeg.

Makes 6

250g/9oz/2¼ cups plain
(all-purpose) flour

250g/9oz/1 cup plus 25g/1oz/2 tbsp
unsalted (sweet) butter

250g/9oz/generous 1 cup curd cheese

25g/1oz/2 tbsp butter

1 onion, chopped

1 small celery stick, thinly sliced

500g/1¼lb minced (ground) beef

6 hard-boiled eggs, chopped

200g/7oz cooked rice (see Cook's tip)

5ml/1 tsp ground allspice

pinch salt

2.5ml/½ tsp ground white pepper

1 egg

beaten egg, to glaze

Cook's tip 150g/5oz uncooked rice
will yield 200g/7oz cooked rice.

Finnish meat pasty
Lihapiirakka

Finnish pies and pasties originated in Russia and were traditionally made with rye pastry and filled with a cooked rice mixture. This recipe uses a rich pastry, made with cheese, and a flavoursome egg and beef filling.

1 To make the pastry, put the flour in a bowl. Cut 250g/9oz/1 cup unsalted butter into small pieces, add to the flour and rub in until the mixture resembles fine breadcrumbs. Alternatively put the flour in a food processor, add the butter and, using a pulsating action, blend to form fine breadcrumbs. Mix in the curd cheese and form the dough into a ball. Leave to rest.

2 Melt the remaining butter in a pan, add the onion and celery and fry for about 5 minutes, until softened. Add the beef and fry, stirring occasionally, until browned.

3 Turn the mince mixture into a bowl. Stir in the hard-boiled eggs, rice, allspice, salt and pepper. Add the raw egg and mix to bind the mixture together.

4 Preheat the oven to 200°C/400°F/Gas 6. On a lightly floured surface, roll out the pastry into six 10cm/4in rounds. Brush the edges with water and place a tablespoonful of the filling in the centre of each round. Fold the pastry over the filling to make a pasty and crimp the edges to seal in the filling.

5 Place the pasties on a baking tray and brush with beaten egg to glaze. Bake in the oven for about 30 minutes, until golden brown. Serve warm.

Per portion Energy 849kcal/3532kJ; Protein 34.1g; Carbohydrate 45.3g, of which sugars 3g; Fat 61.1g, of which saturates 33.6g; Cholesterol 348mg; Calcium 162mg; Fibre 1.5g; Sodium 602mg.

Calf's liver with mustard sauce
Vasikanmaksa sinappikastikkeessa

Veal produces the finest and most delicate offal, so avoid cooking it for too long. If you like the taste of calf's liver, then slice it thickly so that the flavour is more pronounced. Thinner slices will have a less strong taste and will give a crisper outer coating in relation to its soft interior. The creamy sauce enhances the flavour and velvet-like texture of the liver, and the sweet raisins contrast beautifully with the piquant mustard.

1 Put the white wine, stock or water and the sultanas in a pan, bring to the boil then remove from the heat and set aside.

2 Heat the oil and butter in a large frying pan, add the liver slices and fry them for about 2 minutes on each side, until cooked on the inside but still pink in the centre.

3 Using a slotted spoon, transfer the liver from the pan to some kitchen paper and keep warm in a medium oven.

4 Add the shallot and celery to the frying pan and fry for about 5 minutes, until softened, then add the mustard.

5 Strain the white wine into the pan through a sieve (strainer), reserving the sultanas to garnish. Bring to the boil, stirring to deglaze the pan and scraping up any sediment from the bottom of the pan. Stir in the crème fraîche.

6 Pour the wine mixture into a blender or food processor, add the unsalted butter and blend until smooth.

7 Serve the liver on warmed serving plates, scatter over the reserved sultanas and pour over the sauce.

Serves 4

100ml/3½fl oz/scant ½ cup white wine, stock or water

25g/1oz/scant ¼ cup sultanas (golden raisins)

a little olive oil and butter, for frying

4 slices calf's liver, about 200g/7oz each

1 shallot, chopped

1 small celery stick, chopped

15ml/1 tbsp Swedish, German or Dijon mustard

50ml/2fl oz/⅓ cup crème fraîche

25g/1oz/2 tbsp unsalted (sweet) butter

salt and ground black pepper

Cook's tip Calf's liver can be dark or light. The darker the liver is, the stronger the flavour. If necessary, steep the liver slices in cold milk for an hour before use to extract the excess blood. All liver comes naturally encased in a translucent but strong membrane. Carefully remove this as it will shrink during cooking and pull the liver slices out of shape.

Per portion Energy 236kcal/979kJ; Protein 10.1g; Carbohydrate 5.5g, of which sugars 5.4g; Fat 17.7g, of which saturates 8g; Cholesterol 212mg; Calcium 25mg; Fibre 0.3g; Sodium 194mg.

Serves 4

200ml/7fl oz/scant 1 cup water

15ml/1 tbsp salt

150g/5oz/¾ cup short grain rice

1 litre/1¾ pints/4 cups milk

25g/1oz/2 tbsp butter, plus extra
for greasing

1 onion, finely chopped

400g/14oz calf's, lamb's or pig's liver

2 eggs

60ml/4 tbsp treacle (molasses) or dark
corn syrup

100g/3¾oz/⅔ cup raisins

2.5ml/½ tsp dried marjoram

2.5ml/½ tsp ground white pepper

lingonberries or another sharp berry,
such as cranberries, to garnish

Liver, rice and treacle pudding
Maksalaatikko

*This combination of ingredients may seem eccentric, but it tastes magnificent.
The astringency of the liver is balanced by the sweetness of the dark syrup
and raisins, and the finished dish is balanced by sharp lingonberries.*

1 Bring the water and salt to the boil in a pan that has a lid. Add the rice then,
stirring continuously to prevent sticking, boil until the water evaporates. Add the
milk, lower the heat, cover, and simmer for about 30 minutes until cooked through.

2 Preheat the oven to 180°C/350°F/Gas 4. Grease a shallow ovenproof dish with
butter. Melt the remaining butter in a pan, add the onion and fry for 5 minutes, until
softened but not browned. Stir into the cooked rice.

3 Put the liver in the bowl of a food processor and chop until fine but not puréed.
Alternatively, finely chop by hand. Transfer to a bowl. Add the eggs, treacle, raisins,
marjoram and pepper to the chopped liver and whisk together. Combine with the
cooked rice.

4 Pour the mixture into the dish and bake in the oven for 1 hour 10 minutes to
1 hour 15 minutes, until the mixture is firm when you press it with an upturned fork.
Serve hot, garnished with lingonberries or another sharp berry.

Per portion pudding Energy 549kcal/2309kJ; Protein 33.6g; Carbohydrate 70.3g, of which sugars 40g;
Fat 15.9g, of which saturates 7.7g; Cholesterol 493mg; Calcium 426mg; Fibre 0.7g; Sodium 294mg.

Cook's tip The choice of liver will
affect the final flavour but you can use
most varieties, except for poultry livers,
which are too delicate to compete with
the other flavours.

Serves 4

50g/2oz/4 tbsp butter

1 small onion, finely chopped

100g/3¾oz best pork fat, such as back fat or lardons, very finely diced

150ml/¼ pint/⅔ cup pork blood

100g/3¾oz/scant 1 cup rye flour

50g/2oz/½ cup plain (all-purpose) flour

2 eggs

200ml/7fl oz/scant 1 cup lager

2.5ml/½ tsp dried marjoram

2.5ml/½ tsp salt

2.5ml/½ tsp ground white pepper

butter, for frying

For the relish

200g/7oz fresh lingonberries or cranberries

50g/2oz/¼ cup caster (superfine) sugar

Cook's tip If you can find it, you can substitute lingonberry conserve for the relish. It is sometimes available at specialist food fairs or online.

Blood pancakes
Veriohukaiset

The resurgence in popularity of homemade (or at least butcher-made) black pudding means that fresh or dried pork blood can be ordered from most good butchers, and it is this that is used to make these pancakes.

1 To make the relish, put the lingonberries and sugar in a bowl and mash them together. Set aside.

2 Melt 25g/1oz/2 tbsp of the butter in a frying pan, add the onion and fry for about 5 minutes, until softened but not browned. Add the diced pork fat and continue to cook until the fat starts to melt. Leave to cool.

3 Sieve (strain) the blood into a bowl. Add the rye and plain flour and whisk together until smooth, then whisk in the eggs, lager, marjoram, salt, pepper and onion mixture. Leave the batter to rest for 1 hour.

4 Before cooking, whisk the batter together if it has separated. Heat a little of the remaining butter in a small frying pan, then spoon in enough batter to swirl around the base of the pan in a thin layer.

5 Cook until golden brown then slip a spatula underneath and turn over. Cook briefly on the other side until golden brown and crisp. Repeat with the remaining butter and batter to make eight small or four large pancakes. Serve the pancakes hot, accompanied by the lingonberry relish.

Per portion Energy 590kcal/2460kJ; Protein 7.2g; Carbohydrate 47.2g, of which sugars 18.6g; Fat 41.3g, of which saturates 17.8g; Cholesterol 145mg; Calcium 57mg; Fibre 4.3g; Sodium 118mg.

Pork fillet with beetroot and sour cream sauce

Porsaanfilee ja punajuurikastike

Beetroot can produce a lovely pink sauce and their rich flavour contrasts well with the sweet roasted pork. When choosing a joint of pork, select a piece that has a small covering of fat, as this will add flavour to the dish.

1 To make the chicken stock, heat the oil in a large pan, add the chicken wings and fry for about 5 minutes until golden brown on all sides.

2 Add the water, onion and celery, bring to the boil, then reduce the heat and simmer for at least 1 hour. Skim off any excess fat using a slotted spoon, then strain the stock into a jug (pitcher). (This should yield about 500ml/17fl oz stock.)

3 Preheat the oven to 180°C/350°F/Gas 4. Sear the pork in a large frying pan, on its fat side, so that it starts to colour.

4 Transfer to a roasting pan and cook in the oven until tender. The time will vary depending upon the thickness of the joint but allow about 40 minutes. Put the cooked pork on a warmed serving plate and leave to rest.

5 Meanwhile, drain off any excess fat from the pan, then add the stock. On top of the stove, bring to the boil, stirring all the time to deglaze the pan and incorporate any sediment on the bottom of the pan.

6 Add half the beetroot and the sour cream to the pan and bring to the boil. Sieve (strain) or pour the mixture into a blender or food processor and blend until the texture is smooth.

7 Pour the sauce on to warmed serving plates. Slice the pork and place on top of the sauce, then scatter over the remaining beetroot.

Serves 4

600g/1lb 6oz boneless pork fillet (tenderloin) or loin

2 cooked beetroots (beet), diced

100ml/3½fl oz/scant ½ cup sour cream

For the chicken stock

25ml/1½ tbsp vegetable oil

150g/5oz chicken wings

1 litre/1¾ pints/4 cups water

1 onion, chopped

1 small celery stick, chopped

Per portion Energy 252kcal/1056kJ; Protein 33.7g; Carbohydrate 4.8g, of which sugars 4.5g; Fat 11g, of which saturates 5.2g; Cholesterol 110mg; Calcium 44mg; Fibre 1g; Sodium 148mg.

Cook's tip After you have strained the stock from the bones, leave them for a further few minutes. You will find that a small quantity of strong-flavoured stock emerges from the resting bones.

Wild duck with parsnips and sauerkraut gravy
Sorsaa ja palsternakkaa hapankaalikastikkeessa

Hunted during the autumn and winter, wild duck come in several guises, each with similar body shape and flavour, but a large variation in size. This recipe uses mallard, one of which will provide one generous serving or two smaller servings. Served with both mashed and roasted parsnips and a thick sauerkraut gravy, this delectable dish makes an ideal meal on a cold night.

1 Preheat the oven to 200°C/400°F/Gas 6. To prepare the ducks, cut the legs away from the carcasses. Also cut away the wishbone – the bone protecting the arch of the neck under the flap of neck skin. Season the duck legs with salt and pepper. Set aside the breast portions.

2 Heat a third of the goose fat in a flameproof casserole, add the duck legs and fry until browned on all sides. Add the onion and celery and then the beer. Cover and cook in the oven for at least 1 hour, until tender.

3 Meanwhile, prepare the parsnips; divide the parsnips into broad bases and thinner stems. Heat half the remaining goose fat in a roasting pan, add the thinner stems and roast in the oven for about 20 minutes or until crisp.

4 Dice the parsnip bases and put in a pan of water. Bring to the boil, then reduce the heat and simmer for about 20 minutes, until tender.

5 Drain the parsnips, return to the pan and mash until smooth. Beat in the butter and milk, then season with salt and pepper. Set aside and keep warm.

6 Heat the remaining goose fat in a large frying pan, add the reserved duck breast portions, still on the bone, and sear on both sides. Transfer to a separate roasting pan and roast for 15 minutes.

7 Carve the breast portions away from the bone. If they are too underdone, return the carved meat to the oven for a few minutes. Your aim is for quite rare meat.

8 To prepare the gravy, skim any excess fat from the pan in which the duck legs have been cooked. Strain the remaining juices into the pan used to cook the duck breast portions.

9 On top of the stove, bring the mixture to the boil, stirring all the time to deglaze the pan and incorporate any sediment on the bottom of the pan. Add the sauerkraut and treacle and stir together.

10 To serve, slice the breast portions lengthways into thin strips. Place a scoop of mashed parsnip in the middle of warmed serving plates, lay the sliced breast meat across the top, add a roasted duck leg, some roast parsnips and pour over the sauerkraut gravy.

Serves 2–4

2 mallards

50g/2oz/¼ cup goose fat

1 onion, chopped

1 small celery stick, chopped

300ml/½ pint/1¼ cups beer

2kg/4½lb parsnips

25g/2oz/¼ cup butter

15ml/1 tbsp milk

100g/3¾oz sauerkraut

5ml/1 tsp treacle (molasses)

salt and ground black pepper

Per portion Energy 657kcal/2756kJ; Protein 30.5g; Carbohydrate 66.8g, of which sugars 32.5g; Fat 29.9g, of which saturates 11.6g; Cholesterol 138mg; Calcium 254mg; Fibre 23.9g; Sodium 367mg.

Desserts
& drinks

Rice, bilberries & cream cheese

Desserts are not usually a major aspect of the Finnish kitchen in the way they are elsewhere. Instead, the sweet aspect of eating is mainly concentrated on the coffee table, with its range of sweet breads and cakes.

There are, however, a number of delectable desserts to choose from, many of which are based on the availability of seasonal fruits. Finland's harvest of wild berries is incredible in its abundance and diversity, so there will be lingonberries, cranberries, bilberries and arctic cloudberries piled up on the market stalls as well as raspberries, strawberries and currants. The inclination is to not play around too much with this temporary summertime abundance, so there will be simple yet exquisite dessert dishes such as cheese and fruit tarts, soft porridge-like purées and light, frothy berry concoctions such as strawberry snow.

Traditional winter offerings are influenced by the Scandinavian winter, so once the cold weather sets in Finns revert to their traditional warming fare of desserts made with rice and served with jam or dried fruit. Desserts made with dairy products such as cream cheese and beestings, a type of cow's milk, are also common.

Drinks, other than the ubiquitous coffee and increasingly popular tea, include luscious smoothies made using a range of summer berries and yogurt, and tangy, slightly fermented May Day mead, which is often served at parties and special occasions throughout the year.

Serves 4

1 litre/1¾ pints/4 cups water

300g/11oz lingonberries, bilberries or cranberries

150g/5oz/scant 1 cup semolina

about 90g/3½oz/½ cup caster (superfine) sugar

fresh berries, to decorate

Lingonberry and semolina pudding
Vatkattu puolukkapuuro

Depending on its coarseness, semolina can be used to make a range of foods, including pasta, polenta and a number of desserts, as here. Decorate the finished dish with a scattering of lingonberries for a truly stunning finale to a meal.

1 Put the water and berries in a pan and bring to the boil. Strain the liquid into a clean pan. Discard the berries or sieve (strain) them into the liquid.

2 Put the semolina in the pan and, stirring all the time, return to the boil. Reduce the heat and simmer gently for 5 minutes, until the semolina is cooked. Add the sugar according to taste and the type of fruit used.

3 Turn the mixture into a bowl and, using an electric whisk, whisk for at least 5 minutes until light and frothy. Serve in individual serving dishes and scatter over a few berries to decorate.

Per portion Energy 246kcal/1050kJ; Protein 4.4g; Carbohydrate 59.3g, of which sugars 30.2g; Fat 0.8g, of which saturates 0g; Cholesterol 0mg; Calcium 22mg; Fibre 2g; Sodium 7mg.

Cook's tip For added texture and flavour, you can add extra fresh berries at the end of step 2.

Christmas rice pudding
Jouluriisipuuro

Considering that the climate of Finland is not suitable for growing rice, it is surprising that it is a staple food. This rice pudding can be served alongside Dried Fruit Soup or topped with some substantial winter fruit, such as prunes. The scope for adding ingredients, such as almonds or spices, is endless.

1 Put the rice and milk in a pan and bring to the boil. Add the salt, lower the heat, cover and simmer gently for about 1 hour, until the rice has absorbed most of the milk and is almost tender. Stir frequently to prevent the rice from sticking and burning on the bottom of the pan.

2 Add the cinnamon, cream, sugar and almonds to the rice and cook for a further 10 minutes, until the rice is tender.

3 Meanwhile, put the prunes and brandy in a pan and heat gently. Serve the rice in individual serving bowls and spoon the prunes on top.

Per portion Energy 617kcal/2577kJ; Protein 14.7g; Carbohydrate 54.9g, of which sugars 36.8g; Fat 35.7g, of which saturates 20.2g; Cholesterol 86mg; Calcium 419mg; Fibre 1.9g; Sodium 145mg.

Serves 4

90g/3½oz/½ cup short grain rice

1.2 litres/2 pints/5 cups milk

pinch of salt

15ml/1 tbsp ground cinnamon

200ml/7fl oz/scant 1 cup double (heavy) cream

50g/2oz/¼ cup caster (superfine) sugar

25g/1oz/¼ cup toasted flaked (sliced) almonds

To serve

100g/3¾oz/scant ½ cup prunes

50ml/2fl oz/¼ cup brandy

Cook's tip A blanched almond, pressed into the rice pudding, in a similar way to a sixpence in a Christmas pudding, is meant to bring good luck to whoever finds it.

Åland island pancake
Ahvenanmaan pannukakku

The Åland islands lie in the Baltic Sea between Sweden and Finland. Like much of western Finland, the islanders are Swedish speaking, and have a distinctive cooking heritage that reflects their varied history of rule by Danes, Swedes, Russians and Finns. For this dessert, think of a batter or rice pudding rather than the thin wafers we normally associate with the word pancake. Serve warm with jam or fresh berries when they are in season.

1 Put the water and rice in a pan, bring to the boil, then reduce the heat and simmer, stirring occasionally to prevent the rice from sticking, for about 30 minutes, until all the water is absorbed.

2 Add 150ml/¼ pint/⅔ cup of the milk to the pan and simmer until all the liquid has been absorbed. (The rice will still be quite hard.)

3 Preheat the oven to 180°C/350°F/Gas 4. Generously grease a deep, ovenproof dish with butter.

4 Meanwhile, put the eggs, sugar, flour, salt and the remaining 350ml/12fl oz/ 1½ cups of milk in a large bowl and beat together to form a slack batter. Stir in the partially cooked rice.

5 Pour the mixture into the prepared dish and bake in the oven for 30 minutes, until the mixture is set and the top has turned a light golden colour.

6 Spoon the dessert into individual serving bowls and serve hot, with jam, or fresh berries when they are in season.

Serves 4

150ml/¼ pint/⅔ cup water

50g/2oz/¼ cup short grain rice

500ml/17fl oz/generous 2 cups milk

butter, for greasing

2 large eggs

50g/2oz/¼ cup caster (superfine) sugar

90g/3½oz/¾ cup plain (all-purpose) flour

2.5ml/½ tsp salt

strawberry, raspberry or cloudberry jam or fresh seasonal berries, to serve

Cook's tips

• Short grain rice has a high starch content, which makes the grains sticky when they are cooked.

• To make this dish even more creamy, pour some double (heavy) cream over the hot dessert once you have spooned it into bowls.

Per portion Energy 265kcal/1121kJ; Protein 10.5g; Carbohydrate 46.4g, of which sugars 19.3g; Fat 5.3g, of which saturates 2.2g; Cholesterol 103mg; Calcium 205mg; Fibre 0.7g; Sodium 336mg.

Makes 1 tart

150g/5oz/10 tbsp unsalted (sweet) butter, softened, plus extra for greasing

150g/5oz/¾ cup caster (superfine) sugar

2 eggs, beaten

5ml/1 tsp vanilla extract

grated rind of 1 lemon and 15ml/1 tbsp lemon juice

250g/9oz/generous ¾ cup cream cheese

For the pastry

500g/1¼lb/4½ cups plain (all-purpose) flour

5ml/1 tsp baking powder

30ml/2 tbsp caster (superfine) sugar

150g/5oz/10 tbsp unsalted (sweet) butter

1 egg, beaten

Karelian cheese tart
Rahkatorttu

This light, creamy tart is perfect as an accompaniment to coffee but, topped with summer berries, it can also be served as a fine dessert.

1 Preheat the oven to 180°C/350°F/Gas 4. Grease a deep, loose-bottomed 23cm/9in cake tin (pan) with butter.

2 To make the pastry, sift the flour and baking powder into a large bowl and add the sugar. Cut the butter into small pieces, add to the flour and rub in until the mixture resembles fine breadcrumbs. Alternatively, put the flour, baking powder and sugar in a food processor, add the butter and, using a pulsating action, blend to form fine breadcrumbs.

3 Add the beaten egg to the flour mixture and mix lightly together to form a dough. Pat the dough into the bottom and up the sides of the tin.

4 Cream the butter and sugar in a large bowl, then add the eggs, one at a time, and beat until smooth. Add the vanilla, lemon juice and rind, and the cream cheese, and mix gently to combine.

5 Pour the mixture into the pastry-lined cake tin and bake in the oven for about 40 minutes, until set. Leave to cool in the tin before serving.

Per portion Energy 5891kcal/24582kJ; Protein 70g; Carbohydrate 578.4g, of which sugars 197.4g; Fat 382.9g, of which saturates 234.6g; Cholesterol 1258mg; Calcium 1151mg; Fibre 15.5g; Sodium 2734mg.

Bilberry tart
Mustikkapiirakka

Bilberries are wild blueberries. They are a seasonal fruit and are not always available, so use the cultivated ones if necessary. The rich, crumbly pastry is made with cream as well as butter, which makes it quite soft to handle, so be sure to rest it well before rolling out and baking.

1 To make the pastry, put the butter in a large bowl and beat until creamy. Add the egg and cream and mix together, then add the flour and mix to form a dough. Cover and leave to rest in the refrigerator for 3–4 hours or, preferably, overnight.

2 Preheat the oven to 200°C/400°F/Gas 6. Put the bilberries, potato flour and sugar in a bowl and mix together.

3 On a lightly floured surface, roll out the pastry to a 30cm/12in round, 1cm/½in thick. Place on a baking sheet and spoon the bilberry mixture on top, leaving a border around the edges. Bake in the oven for about 30 minutes.

Per portion Energy 2266kcal/9452kJ; Protein 29.3g; Carbohydrate 190.7g, of which sugars 83.5g; Fat 159.2g, of which saturates 97.2g; Cholesterol 579mg; Calcium 435mg; Fibre 19.2g; Sodium 1016mg.

Makes 1 medium tart

600g/1lb 6oz bilberries

15ml/1 tbsp potato flour

50g/2oz/¼ cup caster (superfine) sugar

For the pastry

150g/5oz/10 tbsp unsalted (sweet) butter

1 egg

50ml/2fl oz/¼ cup double (heavy) cream

125g/4¼oz/generous ½ cup plain (all-purpose) flour

Cook's tip The function of the potato flour is to soak up any excess juice from the berries as they cook. If preferred, substitute 30ml/2 tbsp ground biscuits (cookies).

Serves 4

20g/¾oz/1½ tbsp butter

2.5ml/½ tsp salt

1 litre/1¾ pints/4 cups beestings

To serve

caster (superfine) sugar

ground cinnamon

Beestings pudding
Uunijuusto

Beestings is an age-old ingredient, still easily obtained in cattle and dairy farming regions around the world. It is the first milk produced by a cow after calving and is thicker, richer and creamier than ordinary milk.

1 Preheat the oven to 200°C/400°F/Gas 6. Grease a 1.5 litre/2½ pint deep, ovenproof dish with the butter. Mix the salt with the beestings, then pour into the prepared dish.

2 Bake in the oven for 35–40 minutes, until set. Serve hot, cut into slices and dusted with sugar and cinnamon.

Per portion Energy 202kcal/838kJ; Protein 8.3g; Carbohydrate 11.3g, of which sugars 11.3g; Fat 13.9g, of which saturates 8.9g; Cholesterol 46mg; Calcium 296mg; Fibre 0g; Sodium 384mg.

Strawberry snow
Mansikkalumi

Strawberries have a delicate, fragrant taste and most desserts made from them are best eaten soon after they are made. In Finland, the dishes called snows are generally made from fresh berries, such as strawberries and raspberries, but can also be made with apples in the autumn.

1 Put the water in a small bowl and sprinkle in the gelatine. Stand the bowl over a pan of hot water and heat gently until dissolved. Remove the bowl from the pan and leave to cool slightly.

2 Put half the crushed strawberries in a pan and bring to the boil. Remove from the heat, then stir in the dissolved gelatine. Chill in the refrigerator for about 2 hours until syrupy.

3 Pour the cream into a bowl and whisk until it holds its shape. Whisk the egg whites until stiff, gradually adding the sugar as they rise. Fold the egg whites into the cooled strawberry mixture, then fold in the remaining crushed strawberries followed by the whipped cream.

4 Turn into individual serving dishes and serve immediately or chill until required. Serve decorated with halved strawberries.

Per portion Energy 443kcal/1841kJ; Protein 7.8g; Carbohydrate 29.1g, of which sugars 29.1g; Fat 33.7g, of which saturates 20.9g; Cholesterol 86mg; Calcium 56mg; Fibre 0.8g; Sodium 81mg.

Serves 4

120ml/4fl oz/½ cup water

15ml/1 tbsp powdered gelatine

300g/11oz/2¾ cups strawberries, crushed lightly

250ml/8fl oz/1 cup double (heavy) cream

4 egg whites

90g/3½oz/½ cup caster (superfine) sugar

halved strawberries, to decorate

Cook's tip Strawberry Snow freezes well and can then be served as an iced strawberry parfait. All you have to do to make this is spoon the mixture into a loaf tin (pan) lined with clear film (plastic wrap) and freeze for a couple of hours, until it is firm.

Serves 4

60ml/4 tbsp cold water

4 gelatine sheets

60ml/4 tbsp hot water

100g/3¾oz/generous ⅓ cup
cloudberry jam

45ml/3 tbsp Lakka (Finnish
cloudberry liqueur)

100g/3¾oz cloudberries or
cloudberry jam

100g/3¾oz/scant 1 cup cream cheese

200ml/7fl oz/scant 1 cup double
(heavy) cream

30ml/2 tbsp sugar

seeds from 1 vanilla pod

15ml/1 tbsp lemon juice

Cook's tip Gelatine is a setting agent
that is used in a number of desserts,
including jellies and mousses. Sheets
of gelatine require soaking before being
combined with other ingredients. You
should never add it directly to boiling
liquid as this impairs its setting qualities.

Cloudberry mousse
Lakkavanukas

The Arctic cloudberry is a close relative of the raspberry. They are golden-yellow in colour and grow naturally in the high northern hemisphere – Finland, Russia and Canada. The Inuits made use of their high vitamin C content to ward off scurvy and the leaves are said to have medicinal properties. As well as eating them raw and in jams, Finns make a sweet liqueur called Lakka from the berries, which can also be used to sweeten recipes.

1 Put 30ml/2 tbsp of the cold water in a bowl, add two gelatine sheets and leave to soak for 5 minutes. Squeeze the sheets into a bowl, add 30ml/2 tbsp of the hot water and stir until dissolved.

2 Put the cloudberry jam and liqueur in a bowl and mix to combine, then mix in the dissolved gelatine. Stir in the berries or the jam.

3 Beat the cream cheese in a large bowl. Pour the double cream into a separate bowl and whisk until it holds its shape. Fold into the cream cheese with the sugar, vanilla seeds and lemon juice.

4 Soak the remaining two gelatine sheets in the remaining 30ml/2 tbsp cold water. Squeeze the sheets into a bowl, add the remaining 30ml/2 tbsp of the hot water and stir until dissolved. Stir the dissolved gelatine into the cream mixture.

5 Put both the mixtures in the refrigerator for an hour or until setting point is reached. Meanwhile, line four large ramekin dishes with clear film (plastic wrap).

6 Just before the mixtures sets, spoon alternate layers of each mixture into the prepared ramekin dishes. Return to the refrigerator and leave to set. To serve, turn out of the dishes on to individual serving plates.

Per portion Energy 501kcal/2082kJ; Protein 5.3g; Carbohydrate 30.8g, of which sugars 30.8g; Fat 38.8g, of which saturates 24.2g; Cholesterol 92mg; Calcium 63mg; Fibre 0.6g; Sodium 96mg.

Serves 4

150g/5oz/scant 1 cup good-quality
mixed dried fruit

1 litre/1¾ pints/4 cups water

100g/3¾oz/generous ½ cup sugar

1 cinnamon stick

15ml/1 tbsp potato flour

15ml/1 tbsp lemon juice

Dried fruit soup
Sekahedelmäkeitto

Dried fruits are regularly sold as mixed selections in Finnish stores, but the combination of fruits is entirely your own choice. A selection of prunes, sultanas and apples is particularly good. The soup is served with whipped cream or to accompany Christmas Rice Pudding as a Christmas treat.

1 Put the dried fruit, water and sugar in a pan and leave to soak overnight or for about 12 hours.

2 Add the cinnamon stick to the pan, bring to the boil, then lower the heat and simmer for 15 minutes. Remove and discard the cinnamon. Using a slotted spoon, transfer the fruit to a serving bowl.

3 Put the potato flour in a bowl and add enough water to form a paste. Bring the cooking liquid to the boil, then stir a little into the paste. Add the potato flour mixture to the pan and, whisking all the time, bring to the boil until lightly thickened. Add the lemon juice, then pour into a bowl and leave to cool. Serve cold.

Per portion Energy 213kcal/908kJ; Protein 1.3g; Carbohydrate 54.7g, of which sugars 51.7g; Fat 0.2g, of which saturates 0g; Cholesterol 0mg; Calcium 42mg; Fibre 0.9g; Sodium 20mg.

Cook's tip Potato flour is often sold under French or Italian names, such as "fecule de pommes de terre", or "farina di patate". Cornflour (cornstarch) can be used as a substitute if you like, but is not a traditional ingredient.

Bilberry smoothie
Mustikkasmoothie

This easy-to-prepare dessert drink combines sweet banana, creamy yogurt and slightly tart bilberries to create a stunning smoothie. Bilberries are ideal, but you could also use blueberries, or a combination of your favourite summer berries, such as raspberries or strawberries.

1 Peel the banana, break it up and put in a liquidizer. Add the yogurt, bilberries and sugar and blend together until smooth.

2 Spoon the smoothie into four glasses and serve with Almond Biscuits.

Per portion Energy 144kcal/611kJ; Protein 8.1g; Carbohydrate 26.5g, of which sugars 26g; Fat 1.6g, of which saturates 0.8g; Cholesterol 2mg; Calcium 268mg; Fibre 2.7g; Sodium 108mg.

Serves 4

1 banana

500ml/17fl oz/generous 2 cups natural (plain) yogurt

400g/14oz/3½ cups bilberries

30ml/2 tbsp sugar

Almond Biscuits (Manteliässät), to serve

May Day mead
Sima

Sima is served on May Day, along with the sweet, crisp doughnuts, called May Day fritters (tippaleivat), and thereafter whenever you fancy. After combining tart lemon juice and rind with sugar and plump raisins, leave the mixture to ferment and become slightly alcoholic. It is very easy to make, and is ideal for sharing with friends and family at special occasions.

1 Peel the yellow rind of the lemons into strips, trying to avoid including any of the white pith.

2 Carefully cut away the bitter pith from the juicy lemon flesh, then cut the flesh into slices.

3 Bring the water to the boil, then stir in the demerara sugar, 100g/3¾oz of the caster sugar and the lemon rind and flesh. Leave to cool.

4 When the liquid is warm to the touch, add the yeast. Leave at room temperature for 8 hours or overnight. By this time it should bubble slightly.

5 Divide the remaining sugar and the raisins between sterilized bottles or jars, then strain the liquid in on top.

6 Cork or seal the bottles tightly, then leave at room temperature until the Sima has fermented and is ready to drink. This will depend on the room temperature and can vary from 6–8 hours to as long as 48 hours. It is ready when the raisins rise to the top of the bottles or jars. Chill in the refrigerator until ready to serve.

Serves 4

2 unwaxed lemons

4 litres/7 pints/16 cups water

150g/5oz/¾ cup demerara (raw) sugar

150g/5oz/¾ cup caster (superfine) sugar

pinch of dried yeast

15ml/1 tbsp raisins

Cook's tips

• Take care that the yeast is added only when the liquid is lukewarm. A little warmth stimulates the yeast into action but too much will kill it.

• If you cannot find unwaxed lemons, use standard ones, but scrub the skins well with hot water to remove the wax coating before using.

Per portion Energy 306kcal/1304kJ; Protein 0.5g; Carbohydrate 81g, of which sugars 81g; Fat 0g, of which saturates 0g; Cholesterol 0mg; Calcium 42mg; Fibre 0.1g; Sodium 7mg.

Baking

Spices, jam & breads

Bread is a staple of Finnish cooking and, along with potatoes, it forms the standard carbohydrate accompaniment for any meal. The different types of bread on offer are based on the type of crop that can be grown locally. Rye and barley, for instance, grow well in the Finnish climate, so the majority of traditional baking is based on these grains. Wheat was, and is, an import that was used for fancy cake-making and dainty breads, but which until modern times didn't form a significant part of the country's diet.

Most traditional savoury breads are rye-based. A starter made from a sour dough is used to aerate the dough, rather than yeast, and will give a satisfying chewy texture to complement the sweetish rye flavour. Hard breads made this way will keep for months. In Western Finland especially, the bread was often made with a central hole, so that it could be kept on a wooden pole until needed.

In Finland, sweet wheat breads take centre stage at the coffee table. This is a spread that is laid on to signify some special occasion, and comprises coffee and a wide selection of baked items. Coffee is the hot drink of choice for Finns, who prefer a mild but full-flavoured blend and roast. The cakes and breads that go with this coffee are significant. Initially, and almost universally, there will be pulla, a braided, cardamom-flavoured, sweet bread. Afterwards, there may be half a dozen tarts, cakes or cheesecake. Guests will be expected to taste them all. This will be no hardship, as the quality of the baking will be a question of pride for the host.

100ml/3½fl oz/scant ½ cup golden (light corn) syrup

5ml/1 tsp grated orange rind

5ml/1 tsp ground cinnamon

2.5ml/½ tsp ground pepper

2.5ml/½ tsp ground ginger

2.5ml/½ tsp ground cloves

5ml/1 tsp ground cardamom

10ml/2 tsp bicarbonate of soda (baking soda)

100ml/3½fl oz/scant ½ cup double (heavy) cream

200g/7oz/scant 1 cup unsalted (sweet) butter, softened

100g/3¾oz/generous ½ cup caster (superfine) sugar

1 egg, beaten

400g/14oz/3½ cups plain (all-purpose) flour

Christmas gingerbread
Joulupiparkakut

This recipe produces a spicy and authentic gingerbread. Ginger is only part of the flavouring, which may include a combination of cinnamon, pepper, cloves and cardamom, lending a complex and interesting taste to the cookies.

1 Put the golden syrup, orange rind, cinnamon, pepper, ginger, cloves and cardamom in a pan and heat gently until warm. Remove from the heat.

2 Mix the bicarbonate of soda into the cream so that it is evenly distributed. Put the butter and sugar in a large bowl and whisk together until light and fluffy. Whisk in the warm spiced syrup, the beaten egg and cream mixture, until well mixed. Add the flour and mix together to form a dough. Wrap in clear film (plastic wrap) and leave to rest in the refrigerator overnight.

3 Preheat the oven to 200°C/400°F/Gas 6. On a lightly floured surface, roll out the dough to a 3mm/⅛in thickness. Place a sheet of baking parchment over the top of the dough, then turn the dough over so that the paper is underneath. Using a round cutter or shapes, cut out the dough, re-rolling and cutting out the dough trimmings. Place on a baking sheet and bake in the oven for 7–10 minutes, until light brown.

Per portion Energy 1039kcal/4349kJ; Protein 12.4g; Carbohydrate 125.6g, of which sugars 48.1g; Fat 57.7g, of which saturates 35.1g; Cholesterol 188mg; Calcium 193mg; Fibre 3.1g; Sodium 399mg.

Cook's tip Dip the tablespoon in boiling water before measuring the syrup to avoid any remaining on the spoon. You should also measure it straight into the pan in which you intend to heat it.

Makes 1 cake

225g/8oz butter, plus extra
for greasing

4 eggs

225g/8oz/generous 1 cup caster
(superfine) sugar

5ml/1 tsp ground cardamom

5ml/1 tsp ground cinnamon

5ml/1 tsp ground ginger

15ml/1 tbsp grated orange rind

2.5ml/½ tsp bicarbonate of soda
(baking soda)

300ml/½ pint/1¼ cups sour cream

225g/8oz/2 cups plain
(all-purpose) flour

Cook's tip
• Single (light) cream can be
substituted for the sour cream but you
should then replace the bicarbonate of
soda (baking soda) with 5ml/1 tsp
baking powder.
• If you have a kugelhopf mould then
this can be used to give the finished
cake a more interesting shape and
greater presence.

Spice cake
Pehmeä maustekakku

*Finnish home-baking tends to be quite simple and does not often include fancy
ingredients. The addition of various spices, however, elevates the cakes and
bakes, producing delicious and aromatic results.*

1 Preheat the oven to 200°C/400°F/Gas 6. Grease a 23cm/9in loose-bottomed cake
tin (pan) or a standard-size kugelhopf mould with butter. Melt the remaining butter.

2 Put the eggs and sugar in a large bowl and whisk together until light and fluffy.
Add the cardamom, cinnamon, ginger and grated orange rind and stir together.

3 Mix the bicarbonate of soda into the sour cream, then add to the egg mixture.
Finally, add the flour and mix together.

4 Pour the mixture into the prepared tin and bake in the oven for 1 hour, until
brown and a skewer inserted in the middle comes out clean. Leave to cool in
the tin, or remove from the tin and cool on a wire rack.

Per portion Energy 3379kcal/14025kJ; Protein 57.7g; Carbohydrate 191.1g, of which sugars 16.1g;
Fat 271.1g, of which saturates 161.5g; Cholesterol 1421mg; Calcium 767mg; Fibre 7g; Sodium 1777mg.

Runeberg's cakes
Runebergin leivokset

These distinctive, easy-to-make cakes appear everywhere in early February, to celebrate the birthday of one of Finland's most popular poets, Johan Runeberg. Although Swedish, Runeberg spent his whole life in Finland and he is regarded as a national poet. These cakes make a delectable tea-time treat.

1 Preheat the oven to 200°C/400°F/Gas 6. Grease twelve dariol or castle pudding tins (pans). Sift the flour and baking powder together into a bowl. Put the eggs and sugar in a large bowl and whisk together until light and fluffy.

2 In a separate bowl, beat the butter until creamy, then beat in the ground almonds and breadcrumbs. Add the mixture to the eggs and sugar and mix together, then stir in the sifted flour.

3 Divide the mixture between the prepared tins, allowing some room for the mixture to rise. Bake in the oven for 15–20 minutes, until a skewer inserted in the middle comes out clean. Leave to cool in the tins before turning out.

4 Brush the cakes with liqueur to dampen them, and then top each with a teaspoonful of raspberry jam.

Per portion Energy 370kcal/1551kJ; Protein 5.4g; Carbohydrate 43.2g, of which sugars 24.1g; Fat 19.2g, of which saturates 9.3g; Cholesterol 67mg; Calcium 68mg; Fibre 1.2g; Sodium 198mg.

Makes 12

175g/6oz/1½ cups plain (all-purpose) flour

5ml/1 tsp baking powder

2 eggs

150g/5oz/¾ cup caster (superfine) sugar

200g/7oz/scant 1 cup unsalted (sweet) butter, plus extra for greasing

90g/3½oz/scant 1 cup ground almonds

125g/4¼oz/generous 2 cups fine fresh breadcrumbs

about 75ml/5 tbsp almond liqueur, such as Amaretto di Sarone

150g/5oz/½ cup raspberry jam

Christmas stars
Joulutähdet

These pretty pastries are Finland's answer to mince pies, although the prune filling is less sweet than mincemeat and does not include any alcohol.

1 Preheat the oven to 200°C/400°F/Gas 6. Sift the flour and baking powder into a large bowl. Cut the butter into small pieces, add to the flour and rub in until the mixture resembles fine breadcrumbs. Alternatively, put the flour and baking powder in a food processor, add the butter and, using a pulsating action, blend to form fine breadcrumbs. Gradually add cold water and mix until it forms a dough.

2 On a lightly floured surface, roll out the pastry to a square 3mm/⅛in thick, then cut into ten squares. Make a diagonal cut from each corner of the squares towards the centre.

3 Chop the prunes into small pieces. Put a spoonful of chopped prunes in the centre of each square of pastry, then lift each corner of the pastry and fold it over to the centre to form a star.

4 Place the stars on a baking sheet and brush with beaten egg. Bake in the oven for 15 minutes, until golden brown. Cool on a wire rack.

Per portion Energy 155kcal/648kJ; Protein 1.5g; Carbohydrate 14.6g, of which sugars 7g; Fat 10.5g, of which saturates 6.5g; Cholesterol 27mg; Calcium 23mg; Fibre 1.5g; Sodium 78mg.

Makes 10

200g/7oz/generous ½ cups plain (all-purpose) flour

5ml/1 tsp baking powder (baking soda)

125g/4½oz/9 tbsp butter, softened

150ml/¼ pint/⅔ cup cold water, or enough to bind

200g/7oz/scant 1 cup ready-to-eat prunes

1 egg, beaten, to glaze

Cook's tip A little brandy, mixed into the prunes, adds an extra dimension.

Serves 4

100g/3¾oz/generous ½ cup caster (superfine) sugar

100g/3¾oz/scant ½ cup unsalted (sweet) butter

1 egg

100ml/3½fl oz/scant ½ cup sour cream

350g/12oz/3 cups plain (all-purpose) flour

5ml/1 tsp baking powder (baking soda)

90ml/6 tbsp raspberry jam

Raspberry jam biscuits
Vadelmapyörykät

These simple biscuits are given an extra dimension by the addition of sour cream. Make plenty, as they will be popular with all the family.

1 Preheat the oven to 180°C/350°F/Gas 4. Put the sugar and butter in a large bowl and beat together until light and fluffy. Beat in the egg, then mix in the sour cream. Sift the flour and baking powder together, then incorporate into the mixture, which will have a fairly wet consistency.

2 On a lightly floured surface, roll out the dough to 5mm/¼in thickness then, using a floured 5cm/2in round cutter, cut out rounds and place on a baking tray. Leave to rest for 15 minutes.

3 Press the centre of each round with your thumb or the back of a teaspoon, then spoon a little raspberry jam into the indentation. Bake in the oven for 12–15 minutes, until golden. Leave to cool on a wire rack.

Per portion Energy 711kcal/2992kJ; Protein 10.9g; Carbohydrate 110.7g, of which sugars 44.1g; Fat 28.1g, of which saturates 16.7g; Cholesterol 116mg; Calcium 173mg; Fibre 2.7g; Sodium 190mg.

Almond biscuits
Manteliässät

These little almond biscuits can be served as part of a selection with coffee or as an accompaniment to a creamy dessert.

1 Preheat the oven to 180°C/350°F/Gas 4. Put the sugar and butter in a large bowl and beat together until light and fluffy. Add the eggs, one at a time, beating well after each addition, then add the almonds and flour. Mix together to make a dough, then form into a ball.

2 On a lightly floured surface, roll out the dough quite thinly and cut into finger thick strips. Cut the strips into 4cm/1½in lengths and twist each piece into an S shape.

3 Place the strips on a baking tray and sprinkle with caster sugar and nibbed almonds. Bake in the oven for 10 minutes, until just golden brown.

Per portion Energy 188kcal/788kJ; Protein 3.5g; Carbohydrate 22.5g, of which sugars 10.9g; Fat 10g, of which saturates 4.4g; Cholesterol 45mg; Calcium 44mg; Fibre 0.8g; Sodium 58mg.

Makes 20

200g/7oz/1 cup sugar

150g/5oz/10 tbsp butter

3 eggs

100g/3¾oz/scant 1 cup ground almonds

350g/12oz/3 cups plain (all-purpose) flour

To decorate

caster (superfine) sugar

nibbed almonds

Makes 8

100g/3¾oz/½ cup short grain rice

15ml/1 tbsp salt

300ml/½ pint/1¼ cups water

600ml/1 pint/2½ cups milk

For the dough

15g/½oz/1 tbsp butter

100g/3¾oz/generous ¾ cup rye flour

75g/3oz/⅔ cup plain (all-purpose) flour

2.5ml/½ tsp salt

100ml/3½fl oz/scant ½ cup cold water

For the glaze

25g/1oz/2 tbsp butter

75ml/5 tbsp milk

For the garnish

6 hard-boiled eggs

25g/1oz/2 tbsp butter, softened

Cook's tip The thin rounds of pastry are fairly delicate and harden in the air quite quickly. To prevent this from happening, sprinkle them with a little rye flour and stack one on top of the other after you have rolled them out.

Karelian rye pastries
Karjalanpiirakka

These popular pastries are usually filled with savoury rice pudding, although mashed potatoes can occasionally be used. The edges are crimped, some of the filling is left exposed, and they are served warm as part of the coffee table spread, with a large spoonful of chopped hard-boiled egg mixed with butter.

1 To make the dough, melt the butter and put it in a large bowl. Leave to cool, then add the rye and plain flours, the salt and water and mix together to form a dough.

2 Divide the dough into eight small balls and roll out each ball on a lightly floured surface into a 12–15cm/4½–6in round.

3 Prepare the filling by putting the rice, salt and water in a pan. Bring to the boil, then boil for about 20 minutes until the water has almost evaporated. Add the milk, reduce the heat, cover and simmer, stirring frequently to prevent the rice from sticking, for about 15 minutes, until the rice is tender. Leave to cool.

4 Preheat the oven to 200°C/400°F/Gas 6. When the rice is cool, place a heap in the centre of each round of dough. Fold the sides of the dough into the centre so that they do not quite reach each other and some of the filling is left exposed. Crimp the edges and place the pastries on a baking tray. Bake in the oven for 10–15 minutes, until brown.

5 Meanwhile, make the glaze. Melt the butter and stir in the milk. As the pastries are taken out of the oven, dunk them in the glaze, then leave, covered with a dish towel, to soften.

6 To prepare the garnish, chop the hard-boiled eggs and put in a bowl. Add the butter and mix together. Serve the pastries with a spoonful of the garnish spooned on to the centre of each.

Per portion Energy 273kcal/1145kJ; Protein 10.4g; Carbohydrate 30.8g, of which sugars 4.2g; Fat 12.7g, of which saturates 6.4g; Cholesterol 165mg; Calcium 144mg; Fibre 1.8g; Sodium 138mg.

Finnish bagels
Vesirinkilät

Originating in eastern Europe, bagels are a popular snack in Finland. The dough is shaped into a ring and boiled in water, rather than left to rise, and then baked in the oven. This gives a chewy texture to the bread.

1 Put the water, yeast and 1.5ml/¼ tsp sugar in a large bowl and blend together, then leave for stand for 10 minutes, until bubbles form.

2 Add a further 15ml/1 tbsp of the sugar to the bowl with the oil and eggs and stir together. Stir in the salt and half the flour, then slowly add the remaining flour.

3 Using your hands, work in the remaining flour to form a dough. Turn the dough on to a lightly floured surface and knead for 10 minutes, until smooth. Cover, then leave in a warm place for about 1 hour, until doubled in size.

4 Knead the dough again by knocking back and kneading several times, then divide the dough into 12 balls and knead each ball until smooth.

5 Form the dough into rolls, the thickness of a cigar, then loop the rolls into rings. Press the ends together to join them. Alternatively, roll out the dough balls and poke a hole through the centre using your finger or the handle of a wooden spoon. Place the rings on a baking sheet and leave to rise in a warm place for 15 minutes, until doubled in size.

6 Preheat the oven to 200°C/400°F/Gas 6. Put about 2 litres/3½ pints/8 cups water in a large pan and bring to the boil. Add the remaining sugar to the water.

7 Drop 3–4 bagels at a time into the water, boil for 1 minute, then, using a slotted spoon, remove them from the water. Transfer to a baking sheet and brush with beaten egg. Bake for 20 minutes, then leave to cool on a wire rack.

Makes about 12

175ml/6fl oz/¾ cup lukewarm water

1 packet active dried yeast or 25g/1oz fresh yeast

60ml/4 tbsp caster (superfine) sugar

60ml/4 tbsp vegetable oil

2 eggs, plus beaten egg to glaze

5ml/1 tsp salt

450g/1lb/4 cups strong white bread flour

Cook's tips
• The hole in the middle of these rolls will tend to close as they are boiled. Use the handle of a wooden spoon or something similar to keep the centre open.
• Some varieties of flour absorb more liquid than others, so don't worry if you cannot work in all the flour or need an extra spoonful.

Per portion Energy 179kcal/754kJ; Protein 4.2g; Carbohydrate 31.1g, of which sugars 5.7g; Fat 5g, of which saturates 0.8g; Cholesterol 32mg; Calcium 54mg; Fibre 1g; Sodium 177mg.

Vyborg pretzels
Viipurin rinkelit

This recipe is a speciality from the Karelian region, which is now part of Russia, and is named after the province's major town, Vyborg. The pretzels are made with a sweet, spiced dough and are formed into a distinctive round shape. You can make them whatever size you like.

1 Put the milk in a pan and heat gently until just warm to the touch. Put the butter, sugar, cardamom, nutmeg, saffron and salt in a large bowl, then pour over the milk and stir to mix. Leave to cool until lukewarm.

2 In a large bowl, blend the dried or fresh yeast in the lukewarm water. Stir until the yeast has dissolved, then add the milk mixture and eggs.

3 Stir in half the flour then, with your hands, work in the remaining flour to form a dough. Turn on to a lightly floured surface and knead for 10 minutes, until smooth. Cover and then leave in a warm place for about 1 hour, until doubled in size.

4 Knead the dough again by knocking back and kneading for a further 10 minutes. Divide the dough into four pieces, form each piece into a ball, then form the balls into rolls 1m/1yd long.

5 Shape the rolls into an upside down U shape, bring the ends together and twist them over each other. Flatten the ends with your fingers, bring them to the top of the loop to form a pretzel shape, and press to seal.

6 Place the pretzels on a baking sheet and leave to rise in a warm place for about 1 hour, until doubled in size.

7 Preheat the oven to 190°C/375°F/Gas 5. To make the glaze, put the egg yolk and milk in a small bowl and mix together. Brush the glaze over the risen pretzels and bake in the oven for about 15 minutes, until golden brown. Leave to cool.

Makes 4

175ml/6fl oz/¾ cup milk

90g/3½oz/7 tbsp butter

75g/3oz/scant ½ cup plus 2 tbsp sugar

5ml/1 tsp ground cardamom

2.5ml/½ tsp ground nutmeg

5ml/1 tsp saffron threads

2.5ml/½ tsp salt

1 packet easy-blend (rapid-rise) dried yeast or 25g/1oz fresh yeast

60ml/4 tbsp lukewarm water

2 eggs, beaten

175g/6oz/1½ cups plain (all-purpose) flour

For the glaze

1 egg yolk

30ml/2 tbsp milk

Cook's tip You can make more, smaller pretzels by dividing the dough into smaller balls. In general, the smaller the pretzel, the less time they will take to cook.

Per portion Energy 462kcal/1939kJ; Protein 9g; Carbohydrate 59.7g, of which sugars 26.4g; Fat 22.6g, of which saturates 13.1g; Cholesterol 146mg; Calcium 144mg; Fibre 1.4g; Sodium 193mg.

Coffee bread
Pulla

Pulla is the universal accompaniment to coffee in Finland. It is a sweet bread, with a cardamom-scented flavour, and is traditionally plaited.

1 Melt 115g/4oz/½ cup of the butter and leave to cool. Crush the cardamom pods with a pestle and mortar to yield about 5ml/1 tsp powder. Put the dried or fresh yeast in a large bowl, add the water and stir until dissolved. Stir in the milk, sugar, salt, eggs and crushed cardamom.

2 Stir in about one-quarter of the flour to form a batter, then beat until smooth. Add a further one-quarter of the flour and the melted butter and stir well together, then beat until the dough is shiny. Stir the remaining flour into the dough, then turn on to a lightly floured surface and knead until the dough feels smooth and elastic. Cover the dough and leave to rest for 15 minutes.

3 Knead the dough again until it is shiny, then put in a bowl, cover and leave in a warm place to rise for at least an hour, or until doubled in size.

4 Repeat the process by knocking back the dough, kneading well and leaving once more to rise for about an hour or until doubled in size.

5 Grease three baking sheets with butter. Turn the dough out on to a lightly floured work surface and cut into three equal-sized pieces, then cut each of these into three equal-sized pieces.

6 Shape each piece of dough into a ball, then roll into 40cm/16in long strips. Pinch the ends of three strips together, then plait together and pinch the ends to seal. Repeat with the remaining pieces of dough to make three loaves. Place on the baking sheets and leave to rise in a warm place for about an hour or until puffy.

7 Preheat the oven to 200°C/400°F/Gas 6. Brush the loaves with beaten egg to glaze and sprinkle with sugar and almonds. Bake in the oven for 25 minutes until golden brown. Serve warm, cut into slices.

Makes 3 loaves

115g/4oz/½ cup butter, plus extra for greasing

10 cardamom pods, seeded

120ml/4fl oz/½ cup lukewarm water

1 packet easy-blend (rapid-rise) dried yeast or 25g/1oz fresh yeast

475ml/16fl oz/2 cups milk

200g/7oz/1 cup caster (superfine) sugar

5ml/1 tsp salt

4 eggs, beaten

900g/2lb/8 cups plain (all-purpose) flour

beaten egg, to glaze

sugar and nibbed almonds, to decorate

Cook's tip

• If you do not want to plait the bread, then shape the dough into three large, round bun shapes. It will not have the visual impact of the plaited loaves, but will still taste delicious.

• These loaves freeze well. To serve, simply defrost completely and then warm in the oven for about 10 minutes before serving.

Per portion Energy 1742kcal/7360kJ; Protein 42.5g; Carbohydrate 310.4g, of which sugars 81.8g; Fat 45.5g, of which saturates 24.3g; Cholesterol 345mg; Calcium 690mg; Fibre 9.3g; Sodium 1062mg.

Easter bread
Pääsiäisleipä

Easter breads tend to be rich and sweet, and come as a relief after the often rather plain Lenten dishes. This Karelian version, like most Easter breads found in Finland, originated in Russia, and is delicious at any time of the year.

1 Put the milk in a pan and heat gently until just warm to the touch. Remove from the heat. In a large bowl, blend the yeast in the lukewarm water, stir until the yeast has dissolved, then add two-thirds of the milk. Sift a quarter of the flour into the yeast mixture and beat until smooth. Leave in a warm place for about 45 minutes, until risen.

2 Melt the butter. Put the egg yolks and sugar in a bowl and whisk together until light and fluffy. Add this to the risen flour mixture and mix together. Add the salt, cardamom, orange peel, lemon rind, raisins and almonds, then beat in the remaining milk and the butter.

3 Gradually add the remaining flour to the mixture, stirring until a stiff dough is formed. Turn the dough on to a lightly floured surface and knead until smooth. Cover and leave in a warm place to prove for about 1 hour, or until doubled in size.

4 Butter a traditional Russian kulich tin (pan) or a deep cake tin. Alternatively, to allow the bread to reach its maximum potential height, use three empty cans or one large coffee can from which the rims have been cut off. Dust the insides of the tins or cans with sugar, then fill halfway with the dough. Leave in a warm place for about an hour or until the dough has risen to the top of the tins.

5 Preheat the oven to 180°C/350°F/Gas 4. Bake the bread in the oven for about 1 hour, until golden brown and a skewer inserted in the middle comes out clean. Leave to cool in the baking tins before turning out.

6 To make the icing, mix the icing sugar and water together. Drizzle the icing across the loaves. To serve, slice off the iced top and cut into slices. Cut the remaining bread in half lengthways and then into slices widthways and arrange in the centre of a large serving dish. Arrange the iced slices around the top.

Makes 3 small or 1 very large loaf

720ml/1 pint 4fl oz/scant 3 cups milk

2 packets easy-blend (rapid-rise) dried yeast

60ml/4 tbsp lukewarm water

800g/1¾lb/7 cups plain (all-purpose) flour

225g/8oz/1 cup unsalted (sweet) butter, plus extra for greasing

4 egg yolks

200g/7oz/1 cup caster (superfine) sugar, plus extra to dust

5ml/1 tsp salt

10ml/2 tsp crushed or ground cardamom

45ml/3 tbsp candied orange peel, chopped

15ml/1 tbsp grated lemon rind

75g/3oz/½ cup raisins, chopped

75g/3oz/½ cup nibbed almonds

For the icing

200g/7oz/1¾ cups icing (confectioners') sugar

60ml/4 tbsp water

Per portion Energy 2440kcal/10278kJ; Protein 44.1g; Carbohydrate 386.2g, of which sugars 182.3g; Fat 90.7g, of which saturates 45.4g; Cholesterol 443mg; Calcium 868mg; Fibre 11.3g; Sodium 646mg.

Suppliers

Internet suppliers

www.amazon.com
www.deli-shop.com
www.igourmet.com
www.nordicdelicatessen.com
www.suomikauppa.fi

Australia

www.igourmet.com/australianfood
See also other internet suppliers
listed above.

Finland

Finnish Food Network
(Online food shop)
Ruokanet Oy, Teknologiapuisto
PL 116, 87400 KAJAANI
Finland
Tel: 358 (0) 86134 340
www.finnishfood.net

Juustosoppi
(Cheese shop)
Kauppahalli, Hämeenkatu 19,
Tampere, 33200
Finland
Tel: 358 3 222 6463

Sweden

The Northerner
(gifts, food and crafts)
Flöjelbergsgatan 16A
43135 Mölndal, Sweden
Tel: 007 812 272 57 37
www.northerner.com

United Kingdom

Nordic
(Scandinavian bar and restaurant)
25 Newman St,
London, W1T 1PN
Tel: 020 7631 3174
www.nordicbar.com

Scandelicious
Visit: Scandelicious at
Borough Market
Southwark Street
London SE1 9AB

Contact: Scandelicious
4 Beaconsfield Road, Aldeburgh
Suffolk IP15 5HF
Tel: 01728 452880
www.scandelicious.co.uk

The Finnish Church in London
(Cafeteria, hostel, shop and sauna)
Swedish Seamens Church
120 Lower Road, Rotherhithe
London SE16 2UB
United Kingdom

United States

Home Baking Co.
(Finnish bakery)
2845 Marine Drive,
Astoria, Oregon 97103
Tel: 001 503 325 4631
imports@andersonbutik.com
www.andersonbutik.com

Berolina Bakery Pastry Shop
(Cakes, pastries and fresh bread)
3421 Ocean View Blvd
Glendale, CA 91208
Tel: 001 (818) 249 6506

Danish Delight Bakery
(Scandinavian breads and
pastries)
3053 Callie Still Road
Lawrenceville, GA 30045
Tel: 001 (770) 466-4437
www.danishdelightbakery.com

Finnishgifts
(Specializing in everything from
Finland, including food)
Gaviidae Common – Skyway
Level, 651 Nicollet Mall,
Minneapolis, Minnesota 55402
Tel: 1-866-346-6474
www.finnishgifts.com

Genuine Scandinavia, LLC.
(Kitchenware, crockery and
accessories)
958 Washington Street, #9
Denver, CO 80203
Tel: 001 (303) 318 0714
Sales@GenuineScandinavia.com
www.GenuineScandinavia.com

The Gift Chalet
(Specializing in everything from
Scandinavia, including food)
8 Washington Street – Route 20
Auburn, MA 01501
Tel: 001 (508) 755-3028
GiftChalet@aol.com
www.giftchaletauburn.com

Nordic Fox
(Restaurant featuring
Scandinavian foods)
10924 Paramount Blvd
Downey, CA 90241
Tel: 001 (562) 869 1414
www.restaurant.com/nordicfox/

Nordic House
(Scandinavian food books
and gifts)
3421 Telegraph Avenue
Oakland, CA 94609
Tel: 001 (510) 653-3882
pia@nordichouse.com
www.nordichouse.com

Norwill
(Scandinavian food)
1400 East Hillsboro Blvd #200
Deerfield Beach FL 33441
Tel: 001 (866) 598 4506
www.norwill.com

Olson's Delicatessen
(Scandinavian foods and gifts)
5660 West Pico Blvd
Los Angeles, CA
Tel: 001 (323) 938 0742

Scandia Food & Gifts Inc.
30 High Street,
Norwalk, CT 06851
Tel: 001 (203) 838 2087
www.scandiafood.com

Scandinavian Marketplace
PO Box 274, 218 Second
Street East, Hastings, MN 55033
Tel: 001 (800) 797-4319
steve@scandinavianmarket.com
www.scandinavianmarket.com

Simply Scandinavian Foods
99 Exchange Street
Portland, ME 04101
Tel: 001 (207) 874 6759;
001 (877) 874 6759 (toll free)
www.simplyscandinavian.com

Touch of Finland
(Internet food market)
2853 US-41 Marquette,
Michigan 49855
www.touchoffinland.com

Wikström's Gourmet Food
(Scandinavian food and gifts)
5247 North Clark Street
Chicago, IL 60640
Tel: 001 (773) 275 6100
www.wikstromsgourmet.com

Index

Picture credits

The publisher would like to
thank the following for the use of
their pictures in the book (l=left,
r=right, t=top, b=bottom). Alamy
13tr. Corbis 6; 7tr; 7cr; 8; 9;
10; 11; 15; 17tc. 4Corners
Images 13tl; 16bl. Rex Features
12; 14; 16tc; 17tr.